THE
MANAGEMENT
COMPASS

Steering the Corporation
Using Hoshin Planning

Michele L. Bechtell

AMA Management Briefing

AMA MEMBERSHIP PUBLICATIONS DIVISION
AMERICAN MANAGEMENT ASSOCIATION

For information on how to order additional copies of this publication, see page 159.

Library of Congress Cataloging-in-Publication Data

Bechtell, Michele L., 1956–
    The management compass : steering the corporation using hoshin planning / Michele L. Bechtell.
      p. cm.—(AMA management briefing)
   ISBN 0-8144-2358-2
   1. Total quality management. 2. Business planning. 3. Strategic planning. I. Title. II. Series.
   HD62.15.B428 1995
   658.4'012—dc20   *95-6292*
                                                  CIP

This Management Briefing has been distributed to all members enrolled in the American Management Association.

First printing.

Contents

Imagine

Imagine an organization that knows who its customers will be ten years from now, and knows how it intends to win their business.

Imagine an organization where the president communicates the vital few strategic priorities, and every person participates in defining how his or her work provides a measurable contribution.

Imagine an organization where everybody knows the methods to follow to guarantee that the organization will meet its objectives.

Imagine an organization where employees integrate daily management with contributions towards the long-term strategic priorities.

Imagine an organization where each manager routinely communicates deviations from plan to enable diagnosis and timely corrective action.

Imagine an organization where the key business systems and organizational design routinely adapt to changes in the environment.

Preface

What is hoshin kanri—a new form of karate? An innovative dish at your favorite restaurant? A new physical fitness system sold through television? No, try again: Hoshin kanri is a management methodology to reliably execute strategic breakthroughs. Initially developed in Japan, it is rapidly gaining favor in the U.S. and around the world. If, like many managers, you don't know the first thing about hoshin management, or if you think this is just another management buzzword, then listen up. Your customers, employees, and shareholders are waiting.

Hewlett-Packard, Intel, Milliken, Texas Instruments, Zytec, and Procter & Gamble are among the world class corporations that are currently using hoshin management to link daily activity with strategic objectives. Other organizations, particularly in the health care industry, are running to catch up.

So compelling is the hoshin planning methodology that CEOs and their senior management teams are spending many hours per year refining this strategy management system. Declares Ron McCormick, vice president of the Semiconductor Group at Texas Instruments:

> Using this management system, we reduced our missed deliveries to committed dates by 75% in one year, our manufacturing cycle times by 60% in two years, customer returns by 70% in two years, and product ppm defect levels by 65% over two years. . . . Most importantly, we gained

market share against some of the toughest competitors in the world. We are still stretching toward our vision. But, the way we are going to get there is by continuing to focus and energize the considerable improvement capabilities of thousands of TI employees using this deployment process.

One of the more esoteric and least understood elements of the total quality management (TQM) methodologies, hoshin management provides a disciplined management system to deploy strategic priorities. Whereas many people complain that TQM produces only incremental improvements in products and services, hoshin management practitioners know differently. As any hoshin expert will tell you, strategy implementation is, itself, a process. So, use the same tools and techniques of process control to reliably execute strategic breakthroughs.

A simple concept, hoshin management consists of just a few simple steps: analyze changes in the external environment; select the vital few priorities; create an integrated plan of attack; execute the plan; and regularly review progress for subsequent modifications. Yet, its governing principles can be summed up in two words—focus and alignment.

Hoshin management is an execution tool. It concentrates resources on the vital few strategic performance gaps selected by the leadership of the organization. Traditional strategic planning methodologies set priorities based on changes in the environment, industry, and customer needs. Hoshin planning finds the high leverage points within those priorities that will catapult the organization toward its vision, one which is continually reexamined in light of changes in the environment.

A generally unknown methodology just a few years ago, hoshin management is rapidly replacing MBO (management by objectives) to make top-level goals and objectives comprehensible to senior managers and front-line employees. In many companies, high-level goals are expressed in abstract financial terms. And there is little or no linkage between local objectives and strategic goals. But in hoshin management, every annual objective derives from the long-term strategy and every employee can see the logic. Observes Lois Gold, quality manager of Hewlett-Packard, whose Andover, Massachusetts, plant was among the first American companies to implement this system:

MBO did not force alignment throughout the organization. It allowed each manager to set objectives with their direct reports. But it didn't provide the rigor in terms of identifying the highest level strategic priorities, aligning the organization, thinking through the resource requirements, creating detailed implementation plans, conducting formal reviews, or building accountability. With hoshin planning, it is no longer a matter of identifying some financial targets in November, putting the plan away, taking it out the next year, dusting it off, and then figuring out how close you got.

To learn more about this management system, don't race off to the bookstore. Despite its growing popularity, hoshin management has been shrouded in a cloak of secrecy and technical mumbo jumbo. There exist only a handful of texts and a few isolated chapters in books to assist the practitioner. But these descriptions read more like crossword puzzles, and are generally difficult to decipher, let alone understand.

Many companies are unwilling to share their technique, because when it comes to hoshin management, it is often difficult to separate the content from the methodology. After all, we are talking about how these organizations are outsmarting their competitors. Says a senior executive from one *Fortune* 50 company: "We spent quite a few years getting this planning methodology down. We are just not interested in helping our competitors figure out how to do it."

Despite these obstacles, the following practitioners willingly and generously assisted me in the development of this management briefing:

Dorothy Bellhouse, vice president, Sewickley Valley Hospital,
William Brewster, president, Gulton Graphics Instruments,
Mark DeLuzio, corporate director, Danaher Business Systems,
Warren Evans, senior manager—quality, Intel Corp., and former examiner for the Malcolm Baldrige National Quality Award,
Lois Gold, quality manager, Hewlett-Packard,
David Lord, quality manager, Procter & Gamble,
Ron McCormick, vice president, The Semiconductor Group, Texas Instruments,
John Petrolini, TQM manager, Teradyne, Inc. ,
Carlos Pizano, managing director, Sinclair S.A.,
John Rogers, vice president long-range planning, Zytec, and
Rolf Weber, president, Orenstein & Koppel, Inc.

Certain individuals provided invaluable review, editorial suggestions, and content improvement. For their contributions to my understanding of hoshin management and for their valuable review and commentary on the manuscript, I am deeply grateful to Professor Mauricio Cardinas, Los Andes University; Carole Guinane and Mark Smith of Quorum Health Resources, Inc.; Roger Ward of Ward Consulting Group, and Kristina Wile of Gould-Kreutzer Associates.

Many thanks go to Don Bohl, group editor at AMA, who had the clarity of vision and professional curiosity to advance this topic in his Management Briefing series. Lastly, I am deeply grateful to Andreas Burkart, Cynthia Wood, and Debra Woog for their encouragement, participaton, and enthusiasm throughout this project.

Introduction
An Overview of Hoshin Management

A recent article in *The Wall Street Journal* suggested the demise of the management vision. "Internally, we don't use the word *vision*," the CEO of a large U.S. automotive company was quoted as saying. "I believe in quantifiable short-term results—things we can all relate to—as opposed to some esoteric thing no one can quantify." Echoed the chairman of a large U.S. computer company: "The last thing [we] need right now is a vision." The chairman of a large U.S. software company declared, "Being a visionary is trivial."

Over the last decade, exhortations by Tom Peters, W. Edwards Deming, Peter Senge, and others led thousands of U.S. companies to create compelling visions and empower employees to improve key business systems. Yet, as many leaders know, few of these companies achieved or sustained superior results. In fact, Harvard professors John Kotter and James Heskett surveyed 207 of these companies to find that only 10 had improved their performance as measured by sales, stock performance, and customer satisfaction.

So, what's going on here? Is crafting a vision a thing of the past? Is it a waste of time to envision how your organization will leverage emerging customer, competitor, and technology trends?

Certainly not! A compelling vision consolidates stakeholders' interests. It describes how the leadership hopes to change "business as usual" to ensure the success of the firm over its competitors. The challenge that today's leaders face is how to translate the vision into dramatic *measurable results*.

MEASURABLE OUTCOMES—NOT WISHFUL THINKING

This briefing is not about wishful thinking. It is not about:

- vacuous, empty vision statements,
- top management rallies for customer focus,
- lofty musings by an out-of-touch CEO, or
- unmeasurable motherhood and apple pie ideas.

Likewise, it is not about making minor improvements in business as usual. It is not about:

- empowering employees to make incremental improvements in products and services,
- reengineering business processes of little strategic value to the organization, or
- assigning quality improvement teams to projects that do not result in high gains for the organization.

Nor is this monograph about one-time acrobatics. It is not about:

- downsizing in the name of reengineering,
- arbitrarily nuking old processes in favor of high-tech ones, or
- achieving growth through mergers and acquisitions.

Instead, it is about how to marshall the efforts of hundreds or thousands of employees to close strategic gaps. It provides a benchmark for you and others in your organization to compare how well your leaders:

- align your organization's goals with changes in the external environment,

- identify and communicate the vital few strategic gaps that must be closed to achieve a leadership position,
- link annual objectives with strategic priorities,
- connect daily activity to measurable strategic outcomes, and
- monitor and control the corporate road map.

As Peter Drucker writes in his seminal book, *The Practice of Management* (1954):

> [Employees] often do not know what their management does and what it is supposed to be doing, how it acts and why, whether it does a good job or not. Indeed the typical picture of what goes on in the "front office" or on the "fourteenth floor" is the medieval geographer's picture of Africa as the stamping ground of the one-eyed ogre, the two-headed pygmy, the immortal phoenix, and the elusive unicorn.

This briefing is about making your leadership accountable for establishing, communicating, and managing strategic priorities. In the end, strategy implementation is a process. And just like any other process, it can be made reliable and continuously improved.

FOUR MANAGEMENT SYSTEMS MOVE TOWARD THE VISION

To achieve their vision, many leaders ask employees to try harder and do better. And while these exhortations may result in some small gains, they do not move the company closer to its vision. Incremental improvements may make processes more efficient, but they do not necessarily make the company more effective. Wayne Bernetti, former vice president of Florida Power & Light, the first recipient of the Deming Prize outside Japan, observes:

> After five years' worth of struggling and 415 teams, we had a number of interesting case studies that all senior management could take pride in. There were stories we could tell our regulators, the press, and our customers. Yet there were problems. Our earnings declined, customer complaints were rising rapidly, the cost of operation was going up faster than inflation, we continued to raise rates to our customers, and there were serious operating problems. . . . Quality improvement was not doing what we thought it would. We diagnosed the situation. Everybody was doing well or trying to do well in every conceivable direction, with some

efforts being counterproductive to other efforts. We realized we had failed to focus our efforts on the best places to perform. We had failed to set priorities.

As the leadership at Florida Power & Light learned, an activity-based approach to improvement generates isolated success stories, yet there remain significant gaps in performance. Despite the best of intentions, when employees try to fix everything, they can still miss the essential goals of the business. Many of these gaps are critical to the long-term health of the business.

Other leaders hope to reengineer their way toward the vision. They attempt to replace dysfunctional business processes with more customer-focused and high-tech ones. In the meantime, they still have a company to run. Observes Lois Gold of Hewlett Packard:

> With reengineering, you look at a process and you make a decision as to whether you want to incrementally improve it, or, because it is so broken as a system, you re-conceptualize it. Once you re-conceptualize it, you still have to come back to manage it.

Reengineering horizontal business processes can provide a competitive advantage. Yet the decision to reengineer a process still needs to be driven from somewhere, and once it is reengineered, employees still need to know the vital few strategic priorities. Reengineering is one possible means to close a strategic gap, but there are others.

Companies need a system for setting and communicating direction. Daily management ensures that the organization's key business processes function properly. Cross-functional management controls the handoffs in key business processes, i.e., it manages the white spaces on the company's organization chart. Strategic planning defines the most promising destination. But a special kind of management is needed to steer the corporation in the direction of the strategic targets. (See Figure I.1.) Dr. Kano, professor of management science at the University of Tokyo, Japan, and member of the Deming Prize Committee for quality management, explained these requirements at the April 1994 meeting of the American Society for Quality Control:

> The relationship among policy management, daily management, and cross-functional management can be explained by comparing an organization to a ship traveling on the sea. To move straight at a steady speed, we need the two following activities: One, each department needs to fulfill

Figure I.1. Hoshin management is a system to steer the organization toward its strategic vision.

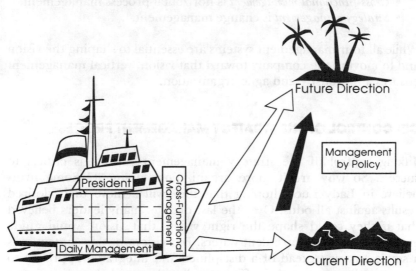

Source: Dr. N. Kano. "Ship" illustration, 1994.

its role faithfully. By this I mean the engine room, the radio room, and the deck. This activity is called daily management, and it is supposed to be done even if there are no specific instructions from the captain. Two, interdepartmental teamwork is necessary. Even though each department performs well, without coordination the ship cannot travel straight at a steady speed. This activity is called cross-functional management.

By conducting these two activities, the ship can move straight at a steady speed in the direction it is currently aiming at. But if the ship needs to speed up or slow down or change direction, the activity to change direction must be enacted according to the captain's instruction. This activity is called management by policy.

Like the captain in this example, most leaders need to steer their organizations through rough waters. In such a climate, static concepts such as daily management and one-time process redesigns are insufficient to manage the journey. Leaders still need a navigational system to steer the organization in the direction that offers the most promising strategic position.

In summary, steering the corporation requires four primary management systems:

- *Strategic planning* is forward management.
- *Daily management* is local maintenance.
- *Cross-functional management* is horizontal process management.
- *Strategy management* is change management.

While all four management systems are essential to shaping the vision and to moving the company toward that vision, vertical management ensures a responsive and agile organization.

GET CONTROL OF THE STRATEGY MANAGEMENT PROCESS

Taking control of the strategy management process is critical to success. So why aren't more organizations doing it? Some firms believe in Lady Luck, hoping that they will achieve their desired results against all odds. Over the last decade, many leaders believed that if they could shape the right vision, that vision would guide employees through turbulent waters. But vision, in this context, was a single answer instead of a disciplined and integrated approach to change. When cause and effect are loosely coupled, management becomes a matter of trial and error. Such an approach to managing time and performance is neither reliable nor replicable.

Other firms are more systematic in managing performance. They attempt to link behavior with strategic imperatives. So, they employ a performance management system called management by objectives (MBO) to control results.

Introduced in the 1950s, MBO was a planning and performance management system designed to steer an organization in the direction desired by top management. In the traditional approach to MBO, top management established an objective—for example, to reduce costs by 30 percent. The target was communicated down the organization in a vertical way to create functional and individual targets. Bosses set targets for their subordinates, and personnel were evaluated on whether or not they met these targets.

A key assumption behind MBO was that one could control results by controlling personnel. By dictating individual targets, MBO assumed that employees would achieve the desired results. And by holding employees accountable for these results, it aimed to motivate employees to improve in every area where performance and results directly and vitally affect the survival and prosperity of the business.

TRADITIONAL METHODS DO NOT WORK

So what went wrong? If MBO intended to translate strategic objectives into measurable outcomes, then why are companies like Hewlett-Packard, Florida Power & Light, Intel, Texas Instruments, and Procter & Gamble replacing their traditional versions of MBO with a new performance management system? The answer is simple. It is not the concept of establishing and tracking individual goals and objectives that bothers them. Rather, it is the *way* in which the objectives and the means to achieve them were developed and deployed.

MBO violates many current principles of management. Whether it is customer focus, employee empowerment, process control, or continuous improvement, key tenets of contemporary management wisdom are conspicuously absent from the traditional MBO methodology. While MBO reflected early management beliefs about how to motivate people and execute strategy, it simply no longer fits in with what we understand today about achieving superior performance. Specifically,

- *MBO relies on one-way communication.* In the traditional MBO planning process, communications primarily go in one direction—from boss to subordinate. There is little input from employees on the feasibility of goals and targets. As a result, plans are often unrealistic and unsupported.
- *MBO relies on management after the fact.* Management by objectives focuses on results. While outcomes do matter, failing to achieve revenue targets, customer satisfaction, or cost reductions are merely lagging indicators of performance. They shed little light on *why* the results were or were not accomplished. As a result, managers rarely catch deviations early and, therefore, rarely fix them.
- *MBO gambles on the individual skills of the personnel.* To maximize performance, MBO cultures invest in individual employees, but expend little or no effort to understand and improve the capability of the system. They fail to systematically improve the cause and effect linkage between local plans and the desired results.
- *MBO fails to eliminate chronic problems.* In MBO, problems are typically identified at the local level: Sales personnel are expected to solve problems that emerge in the sales arena, manu-

facturing personnel are expected to control problems that become visible in their area, and so on. The truth is, a local problem is often merely a symptom of a much more complicated problem involving several departments and issues. The root cause(s) of systemic problems are rarely identified and/or solved.

- *MBO fails to document, let alone capture, knowledge.* In traditional organizations, the performance review is treated more like an annual event than a rigorous feedback loop. The organization rarely transfers local lessons upward in the hierarchy to inform future rounds of planning.

- *MBO is used as a weapon, not a tool.* Too often, MBO is used as a covert—or overt—threat to employees. Measuring the performance of individuals against "top-down" objectives becomes more important than understanding the capability and performance of the management system.

- *MBO lacks vertical and horizontal linkage.* The management by objectives system emphasizes coupling between layers of management. Yet it fails to tie daily activity to strategic requirements. Annual objectives are driven by a budget which is often financially driven, not directly linked to the strategic plan.

In summary, for all its popularity, the traditional management by objectives approach to vertical management frequently fails to provide the leadership and hierarchical responsiveness required to make and sustain dramatic improvement. Simply assigning goals and objectives to members of the organization does not guarantee that they will be implemented or achieved. In the absence of role clarity, attention to means and methods, meaningful measures, and employee commitment, MBO is, by default, MBL, managing by luck—an unreliable and ineffective system.

USE HOSHIN PLANNING TO ALIGN PEOPLE AND ACTIVITIES WITH THE STRATEGIC INTENT

If management by objectives is so deficient in communicating direction and ensuring cross-functional coordination, then how can managers develop, communicate, and monitor their corporate road maps? How can they provide the bite to back up the bark? The answer is to find an alternative management methodology to disseminate and implement strategic policy in a turbulent operating environment. Specifically, it must be able to:

- align the organization with changes in the external environment,
- translate the challenges into a small set of strategic gaps that must be closed, and
- mobilize the entire organization to close these gaps.

Such a planning process already exists. The Japanese call it *hoshin kanri*. The word *hoshin* is formed from two Chinese characters: *ho* stands for "method," *shin* means "shiny metal showing direction." *Kanri* stands for "planning." Together, *hoshin kanri* is used to communicate a "methodology for setting strategic direction," in other words, a management "compass."

To many Western organizations, this goal attainment process is variously called hoshin planning, hoshin management, management by planning (MBP), policy management, and policy deployment. The term "policy deployment" may initially confuse some people: In the United States, policy is frequently associated with government, company rules, and/or management exhortations. But in the context of hoshin management, the word "policy" is used to convey a set of strategic priorities, as well as the means or methods to achieve them. In other words, policy is not policy unless the objectives and the methods are visible as theory in action.

More than a method of telling others what to do, hoshin management is a disciplined methodology to reliably execute strategic breakthroughs. It is that part of the total quality management system which identifies, develops, deploys, audits, and modifies a specific plan to focus the organization on a few strategic priorities. A methodology to manage change, it aligns and coordinates key business systems to achieve specific breakthrough targets.

Hoshin Management Is an Idea Handler, Not an Idea Generator

Hoshin planning is not a strategic planning tool; it is an *execution* tool. It is a system to deploy an existing strategic plan throughout the organization. In other words, it depends on a preexisting statement of direction—a clear set of objectives articulated by the CEO—typically generated by an augmented strategic planning process.

Traditional planning methodologies focus on strategic markets. For example, the question in senior management's mind might be, "Should I make plastic umbrellas or not? Is there a market for them? How big is it? Can I be a dominant player?"

Hoshin management does not answer such big business questions. Instead, it will help you figure out the optimum way to be an umbrella manufacturer, once you decide to be one. It will help you figure out how to focus on the customer and deploy a small set of strategic priorities that support the management vision.

Hoshin kanri translates the strategic intent into the required day-to-day behavior. (See Figure I.2.) It converts the vague generalities of long-term objectives into a set of ambitious but realistic short-term strategies that the organization can act upon. John Rogers observes:

> Management by Planning, as conceived by Zytec, is unabashedly practical. There are many good strategic planning systems that concentrate on the generation of ideas. So, our system concentrates on the conversion of good ideas into executable actions that can be carried out at all levels of the company.

Figure I.2. Strategy management is needed in addition to strategic planning.

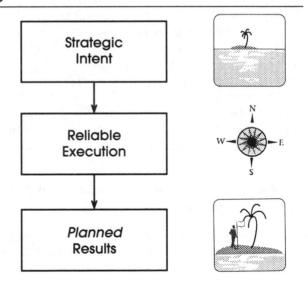

In this way, hoshin planning is a complement to, not a replacement for traditional strategic planning. Whereas traditional strategic planning identifies the organizational priorities based on changes in the environment, customer needs, and technology, hoshin planning provides a systematic methodology to identify the high leverage points within those priorities.

What Does Hoshin Planning Look Like?

Hoshin management is not another attempt to improve MBO. While hoshin management and MBO both aim to deploy company goals and encourage employees to achieve them, there are several radical points of departure. Specifically,

- *Hoshin management deploys the voice of the customer, not just profit goals.* More than the traditional MBO description of projected market share, profit goals, and revenues, hoshin management maps and controls the path to a new design based on customer priorities. It describes the behaviors needed to achieve the policies that support the strategic vision.
- *Hoshin management deploys breakthrough strategies.* It concentrates resources on strategic priorities and chronic problems by going after the root cause(s) of obstacles to achieve dramatic improvements in performance.
- *Hoshin management controls the means and methods, not just the results.* It manages the cause and effect linkage of supporting strategies, measures, and targets to ensure that employee efforts are realistic, synergistic, and add up to the total effort required to meet corporate objectives.
- *Hoshin management is a continuous management process, not a calendar-driven system.* MBO typically establishes a set of quarterly and annual goals. In contrast, hoshin management identifies a few critical breakthrough objectives that require coordinated and focused effort over an extended period of three to five years. Annual objectives are established within the context of these longer term objectives.
- *Hoshin management emphasizes frequent reviews up and down the organization.* In MBO, the performance review, often an annual event, does not capture or communicate valuable feedback to inform future rounds of planning. Hoshin management uses an

explicit inter-level communication system to continually distill local lessons and channel them upward to the leaders of the organization. It routinely tracks performance, reviews the capability of the entire planning system, and modifies it accordingly.

- *Hoshin management is not tied to performance appraisals.* Authentic hoshin management separates the evaluation of personnel from the evaluation of the strategy management system. It focuses not on personnel, but on the quality of the strategic assumptions and the discipline of the planning system.

Features like these make hoshin management an attractive replacement for MBO. A new age performance management system, hoshin management uses the latest principles in industrial psychology, organizational learning, system dynamics, and scientific inquiry. It emphasizes modern management principles: customer focus, process control, employee participation, and management by fact.

THE PRINCIPLES BEHIND HOSHIN MANAGEMENT

There are many versions of hoshin management. However, certain themes recur in many stages of the planning process, at many levels of the hierarchy, and at many levels of abstraction. These principles will reappear in various forms throughout this management briefing. (See Figure I.3.) These principles include:

- Align the organization's goals with changes in the environment.
- Focus on the vital few strategic gaps.
- Work with others to develop plans to close the gaps.
- Specify the methods and measures to achieve the strategic objectives.
- Make visible the cause and effect linkages among local plans.
- Continuously improve the planning process.

These principles describe certain basic practices associated with the school of total quality management (TQM). In the context of hoshin management, they are specifically applied to achieving dramatic and measurable breakthroughs.

Let's take a brief look at these.

Figure I.3. Six principles support hoshin management.

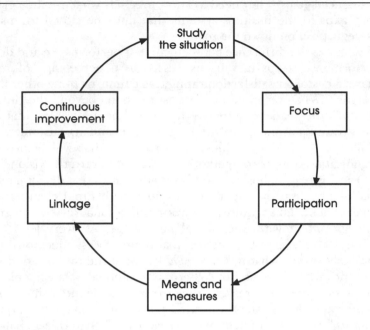

Study the Situation

Too often, executives define their management vision as "being profitable" or "going public." In other companies, annual objectives are stated in enigmatic financial terms, such as "generate a trading profit of 25%." Now, to the average employee, just *what* does that mean? Observes Ron McCormick of Texas Instruments:

> Before we implemented policy deployment [hoshin management], our company was primarily driven by forecasts like, "We are going to make X billion dollars in revenue." Every department had its share of the revenues that added up to the total. All of the staff and support organizations had a financial overhead goal that they had to meet for profitability. But there was no methodology that involved the employees in the initial action program to achieve the plan. As one of our counselors pointed out, it was an annual dream, not an annual plan. We didn't focus the minds and the abilities of thirty to forty thousand people. With policy deployment, we can now focus employees on the things that are most important to the business. We now have a much better chance of hitting our current and future goals.

Employees need more direction than the abstract foreign language of financial goals. They need to know precisely what are the performance gaps in the business systems that must be closed to ensure a strategic position down the road.

A gap is the difference between current performance and desired performance. Gaps may be expressed as a percentage of market share, a customer satisfaction rating, cycle time, or some other unit of measure. Whatever the unit of measure, to get beyond the "financial dream," the leadership needs to select the indicators that offer the greatest advantage to the organization and its customers. The challenge is to identify those opportunities that will leapfrog the organization over its competitors and steer it toward the vision.

For this reason, hoshin management requires that decision makers continually align the organization's goals with rapid changes in the environment. This requires a thorough situational review, integrating strategic intent with operational knowledge. At every level of the hierarchy, at every stage of the planning process, decision makers routinely review what *is*, what *might* be, what the organization *should* do, and what it *must* do. Whereas traditional strategic planning emphasizes *analysis*, breaking down the strategic intent into a set of comfortable linear steps forward, hoshin management starts with *synthesis*, creating an integrated perspective of the critical challenges to the organization.

Focus on the Vital Few Priorities

Hoshin management is a management system to identify and close gaps. Yet some gaps are more strategically important than others. In hoshin management, strategic objectives identify the most critical gaps for the company. Once these are identified, employees can then pinpoint the group, division, factory, department, and project gaps that must be closed to support the overall effort.

A key principle of hoshin kanri is to deploy and track only a few priorities at each level of the organization. Given all of the rapid changes and increasing distractions organizations face today, individuals must be able to focus quickly on those things that offer the greatest advantage to the organization. The clearer the priorities, the easier it will be for people to focus their energies on what really counts.

There are many techniques to identify the vital few factors that cause performance gaps. However, most companies use Pareto analysis to select the starting point for setting priorities. Pareto analysis illustrates that most of our problems are caused by a handful of factors: perhaps 80% of our errors are caused by 20% of the sources of variation. In other words, not all sources of error are equal.

Pareto analysis relies on a Pareto chart, a special form of a vertical bar graph, to select which problems to solve in what order. We will gain more by working on the tallest bar than we would if we were to tackle the smaller bars.

While the Pareto chart indicates where to start, not all "fixes" are the same. Addressing a *symptom* of a deeper problem is considerably less effective than identifying and eliminating the *root cause*. Yet, the root cause of a problem is hidden. Fortunately, some simple techniques can be used to identify it. One technique, called the "five whys," is to simply ask "why?" five times, basing each consecutive question on the last "because." By the time you obtain an answer to the fifth "why," you typically arrive at the fundamental source of the problem. Another management tool, the fishbone diagram, can be used to identify and map the multiple contributing factors to a problem.

Going after the root cause barriers to progress offers greater leverage than other courses of action.

Ask Employees to Develop the Plans to Close the Gaps

When it comes to closing strategic gaps, employees are the change agents. So in hoshin planning, top management communicates the vital few strategic gaps, but not how it is going to close them. They invite teams to design their own plans, review their own progress, and communicate with other teams to ensure alignment and coordination.

Knowledge improves the quality of strategic choices. Yet in too many organizations, senior managers treat top level strategies and objectives as confidential: Only an elite group is privy to critical pieces of information. There is little sharing of local information. And power is measured by the extent to which an individual has access to closely held information. Derick Pasternak, MD, President of the Lovelace Health System in Albuquerque, New Mexico, recalls:

We used to be so concerned about the competition getting hold of our strategic plan that we did not distribute it very widely. We changed the process because we found that although top and middle management had a reasonable understanding of the plan, supervisors and front-line physicians barely had any awareness that the plan existed. We really felt the entire organization needed to understand the plan to execute it better. But you can't execute if you don't know what is in the plan.[1]

Inadequate information can wreak havoc on the management system. Without clear communication from the top, employees may be pursuing strategies at the front line that are several years out of date. Unless employees participate in the general dialogue of the strategic planning process, they will be uninformed. And when employees are uninformed of the broader context, redundancies, omissions, and dissension become the norm.

For this reason, hoshin management emphasizes knowledge exchange. First, an explicit inter-level communication methodology disseminates strategic information to inform employees, increase clarity, and negotiate plan details. Second, frequent reviews up and down the organization direct local lessons upward to inform senior management of the realities on the front line. Knowledge *transfer* is a one-way communication from management to the employees. When there is knowledge *exchange*, senior managers exchange their perception of problems with knowledge of a possible solution from employees, customers, suppliers, and others.

Specify the Means and Measures to Close the Gaps

As Peter Drucker notes in *The Practice of Management*, measurement determines what one pays attention to. "It makes things visible and tangible. The things that are measured become relevant; the things that are omitted are out of sight and mind." Taking the time to translate high-level corporate requirements into meaningful measures at the local level helps to ensure that employees attend to the most appropriate tasks, and that the effort meets the requirements.

Too few leaders take this seriously. They have lots of metrics, but they do not link these with strategic priorities, and there is no way to verify that local strategies add up to deliver the required results. In the absence of a set of appropriate, necessary, and sufficient indicators, it is only a fantasy that they are in control of their organizations.

Hoshin metrics are different from those established under MBO.

MBO typically communicates desired annual results like "reduce costs by 30%," but it fails to provide any metrics to responsibly manage the "how" throughout the year. And it fails to link the metrics as the actions roll down the organization. The high-level objective cascades to lower levels of the organization, usually in the same units of measure. The methods and strategies may change on each level of hierarchy, but the metrics do not. In the end, the senior leadership and employees are stuck with a simple, but ineffective, tracking system.

In hoshin management, metrics are customized to fit the means. The truth is, when you achieve a goal, you are actually experiencing the outcome of a whole series of reliable sequences. When you control the methods, you improve the likelihood of achieving the desired outcome. When the methods and measures are linked, you don't just get results, you get *planned* results.

This concept is similar to planning a trip. We are more likely to arrive at our destination if we not only manage by results, "did we get there or not," but also if we use check points along the way. Results, or *control* points tell us whether we achieve our goal after the fact, i.e., whether the process is *capable* or the methods were effectively designed. *Check* points tell us whether we are following our plan, i.e., whether or not the process is *stable* and working as designed.

For this reason, hoshin management goes behind the performance to control the means at every level of the hierarchy. As the annual objective rolls down the organization, strategies are converted into tactics, then projects, then action. The metrics change accordingly so that employees can monitor the results and the behavior that will lead them to the desired results. Every high-level objective is translated into one or more means; every means is assigned a measure or indicator. In this way, words and numbers link the objectives and the strategies. Leaders can verify that the combination of local plans adds up to deliver the corporate requirements.

Selecting measures for means helps to reinforce the concept that strategy implementation is a process—one that can continually be improved through discovering what works, what fails, and why. By tracking the methods, we can validate or revise our working assumptions. We can better understand the capability of the organization— not simply the performance of an individual. And, we can observe deviations from plan and take timely corrective action.

Make the Cause and Effect Relationships Visible

One secret of hoshin management is, quite simply, alignment. Hoshin management aims to:

- Align the organization's goals with changes in the external environment. This ensures adaptiveness.
- Align employees with the key objectives. This builds momentum.
- Align all activities, tasks, and performance metrics with organizational goals. This increases effectiveness.

The result is an organization that consistently focuses on a few priorities, identifies key systems that need to be improved to achieve strategic objectives, and then clearly communicates that focus throughout the organization. By rigorously controlling the cause and effect linkage among people, plans, and activities, the system provides consistent resource allocation in the long term, focus in the medium term, and participation in the short term.

To this end, hoshin planning requires that managers understand the cause and effect relationships that drive their business. It demands that managers take the time to (1) document and study the rationale for their choices, (2) understand the key relationships that generate and control the dynamic process of change, and (3) design their change strategies to reflect their understanding of these relationships.

Hoshin management relies on two sets of tools to make the logic visible:

- One set of tools helps us analyze numerical data. (Appendix A)
- Another set of tools helps organize language data. (Appendix B)

These tools are referenced repeatedly throughout this briefing and all support the principle of "manage by fact, not by myth." The greater extent to which the management vision and supporting long-term plans are grounded in facts and analysis, the more appropriate and robust the resultant strategies.

Iteratively Zero in on Strategic Objectives

At the heart of hoshin management is the Plan-Do-Study-Act (PDSA) cycle. Promoted by W. Edwards Deming, this management cycle (sometimes called the PDCA cycle) is an iterative improvement process. A closed loop system, it emphasizes four repetitive steps:

- First, start with an idea and create a PLAN to test it.
- Then, DO adhere to the plan, and take corrective action when necessary.
- Next, analyze and STUDY discrepancies to identify the root causes of obstacles.
- Finally, take appropriate ACTion. If the outcome matches expectations, then standardize the process to maintain the gains. If the results were disappointing, then modify the process to eliminate the root cause of remaining problems. In either case, repeat the process starting again with PLAN.

While these steps appear in a linear sequence, when implemented the phases are best thought of as concurrent processes that can continually be improved.

The PDSA cycle is used on several levels. The PDSA cycle provides a superb tool for managing strategic priorities. Using the PDSA cycle, members of an organization can repeatedly plan, execute, study, and adjust their individual and organizational behavior to achieve their desired strategic objective. (See Figure I.4.) "Rotation of the PDSA cycle moves the organization closer and closer to its stated goals, objectives, and ultimately the vision," states Roger Ward, formerly of Florida Power & Light. This happens in three ways. The PDSA cycle is used to plan, execute, monitor, and adjust the mid-term strategies (three to five years) toward the long-term objectives. The multiple annual rotations of the PDSA cycle ensure that customer needs are met in a responsive and timely manner toward the mid-term objectives. In addition, a mini PDSA cycle controls the annual plan throughout the year. Said another way, the PDSA cycle ensures three types of improvement:

- *Proactive adjustment:* Leaders use the PDSA cycle repeatedly to modify the intermediate plans to succeed in a dynamic environment, and improve the reliability of the planning and execution system.
- *Corrective action:* Employees use the PDSA cycle to align key business processes with the annual strategic objectives.

Figure I.4. Use the PDSA cycle to achieve strategic breakthroughs.

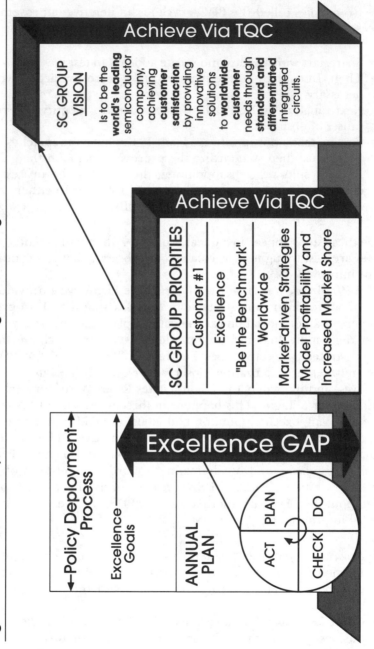

Source: Texas Instruments. Used by permission.

- *Control:* Employees use the PDSA cycle to adhere to the plan, using measurement and standardization to hold the gains.

These three applications of the PDSA cycle make closing strategic gaps an iterative process, rather than an event. It iteratively aligns activities, resources, and results with strategic objectives. John Hudiburg, former CEO of Florida Power & Light, observes in *Winning with Quality*:

> Dr. Asaka likened a company just getting started to a group of arrows dropped on the floor randomly, pointing in all directions. The arrows represent the efforts of the different departments—forceful and well intentioned, but uncoordinated. After the first attempt at policy deployment (that is, the first PDCA cycle), the arrows look like the spokes of a hand-held fan, more or less pointing in the same general direction but still not perfectly aligned. After another iteration of the PDCA cycle, the arrows are parallel and all point in the same direction, but have gaps between them. Finally, after one more turn of the PDCA wheel, the arrows are all aligned in a bundle, mutually supporting each other, with a third dimension—depth. The arrows in the bundle support each other and produce greatly enhanced strength. Likewise, in an organization, the various elements of the company work together cross-functionally to produce greatly enhanced results. Today I use the same description to explain the effects of policy management at FPL.

As Hudiburg and his team learned, the PDSA cycle is an effective tool to improve continuously upon the plans, goals, targets, and even the planning process itself. It forces operating assumptions to be publicly uncovered, documented, tested, and continually revised.

Use the SA-PDSA cycle to manage a dynamic environment. One disadvantage of the PDSA cycle is that, when used on a regular basis, it can cause a manager to focus only on problems identified during the most recent iteration of the improvement cycle. This is not surprising, as the objective of the PDSA cycle is to reduce variance from the ideal target value by eliminating the most important problems, one after the other.

When the target remains constant, the PDSA is a highly effective management tool. But in the face of a changing environment, we are often chasing a moving target. In such a situation, we want to reduce variance from plan. We also need to revise our goals and modify our plans as new developments occur from iteration to iteration. This requires special attention to the Study-Act piece of the PDSA cycle. Recalls John Hudiburg:

> Any organization that has existed for any length of time is probably good at "plan-do"; at FPL we had always done a pretty good job of this. But back in 1985, the "check-act" part was virtually nonexistent. "Check-act," as we came to learn it, means using data to analyze whether the actual results of "do" were the ones planned, and then taking action to improve the next PDCA cycle. (At that time we would have said we did this, but in hindsight it is clear that any attempts we made were pretty superficial.) And PDCA s applied not only to improve problem-solving skills but also to improve the quality improvement process itself; this application is probably the most important use of the PDCA cycle.

For this reason, many organizations begin hoshin management with the STUDY phase of the PDSA cycle. In other words, the system is studied and evaluated before any plans are developed.

The hoshin management cycle is sometimes described as the SA/PDSA (Study-Act/Plan-Do-Study-Act) cycle. In the face of changing goals and moving targets, the SA/PDSA cycle reminds members of the organization not only to review past performance, but also to conduct a qualitative assessment of the next important direction. As the environment changes, the organization can modify its strategic priorities to ensure a dominant position in the eye of the customer.

THE BOOK

In summary, the hoshin management system *is* a management compass. (See Figure I.5) It is a management tool to align people, activities, and performance metrics with strategic priorities. It can be used to communicate direction, coordinate activity, and monitor progress. It enables members of the organization to work together in the most creative way to define and achieve the strategic intent.

To delineate the hoshin planning process, this briefing is divided into six chapters:

- **Chapter 1** describes how to set strategic direction. Before an organization can effectively deploy strategic objectives, top management must first reach a consensus on its strategic intent. It must look

Figure I.5. Hoshin management uses cycles within cycles.

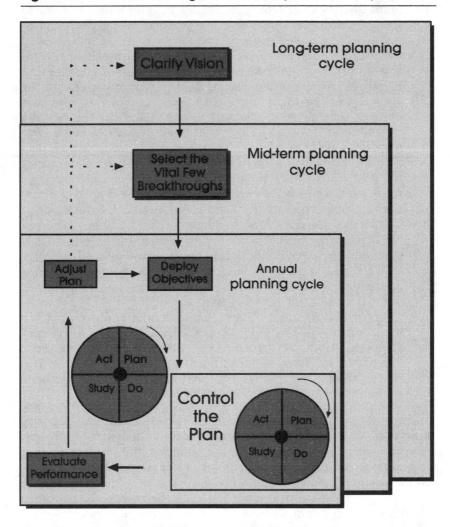

beyond its current problems and successes to identify new opportunities and threats and shape a future of its own choosing.

- **Chapter 2** describes a methodology to define the critical few priorities and/or supporting policies to materialize the long-term vision. Many leaders believe that they can achieve their goals and objectives by asking teams of employees to identify problems and do their best to solve them. But hoshin management goes beyond motivation and a proliferation of teams to focus collective resources on a few performance gaps that must be closed to ensure a strategic position.

- **Chapter 3** describes a process to deploy the strategic objectives. Hoshin management asks employees to identify the means and measures to achieve the results. It then rigorously checks for vertical and horizontal alignment. The rigor of this approach ensures that all supporting plans are based on the realistic capability of the organization and are sufficient to realize the organization's aims.
- **Chapter 4** describes a disciplined management process to control the plan. Plans are rarely achieved with a "hit or miss" management style. So, in hoshin management, employees control deviations from plan through facts and analysis and corrective action.
- **Chapter 5** describes how to monitor performance. Whereas MBO treats the performance review as an annual event, hoshin management demands a formal review process with regular and frequent reviews up and down the organization. Such a disciplined approach to feedback guarantees that what you set out to do, you actually accomplish.
- **Chapter 6** puts hoshin management in the context of other management systems and practices, including total quality management, reengineering activities, and performance appraisal practices. The chapter ends with a few comments about the first steps a company might take in building a hoshin management system.

In the end, strategy implementation is a process. And just like any other process, it can be made reliable and continuously be improved. Driving variability out of the strategic planning and implementation process improves the quality and power of our strategies for competitive advantage. It increases the probability that we achieve what we set out to do. So, where do you start? What are the blueprints that other organizations are using to reliably execute strategic breakthroughs? The following pages answers these questions and more, starting with a look in Chapter 1 at clarifying corporate purpose.

NOTES

1. Quoted from James C. Arvantes, "Integrating TQM and Strategic Planning," *The Quality Letter for Healthcare Leaders,* September 1993, p. 2.

1

Formulate the Challenge:
Align the Organization's Goals with Changes in the Environment

Companies that have risen to global leadership over the past 20 years invariably began with ambitions that were out of proportion to their resources and capabilities. But, they created an obsession with winning at all levels of the organization and then sustained that obsession over the 10–20 year quest for global leadership. We term this obsession "strategic intent." —Gary Hamel and C.K. Prahalad

Leaders steer the organization toward a positive future. It is the responsibility of the senior management team to anticipate the future, select the destination, and navigate an expedient course.

When the leadership takes its first steps toward the future, there is little guidance on what should be done. No one knows precisely what the journey will look like or which aspects of the environment will change.

For this reason, hoshin management uses a systematic process to set the agenda for change. By taking the time to envision the future, detect critical changes in the environment, and evaluate the strategic options, leaders are better equipped to deal with the challenges that can steer their organization in the most promising direction.

PREPARE FOR THE FUTURE

Many managers set stretch targets to encourage employees to prepare for the future and take appropriate action. Yet, too often, goals and objectives merely describe solutions to the problems of the day. They do not leverage tomorrow's opportunities. New problems arise weekly, pushing plans for the future aside. The result is that management never takes the necessary short-term steps to prepare for tomorrow.

To point their organization in the most promising direction, more and more leadership teams are using a three-step standardized focusing process. They look beyond today's problems to redraw the environmental map, chose their destination, and chart a path forward. Pat Weber, co-chairman of Texas Instruments, describes his company's three-step direction-setting process.

> A good part of the credit can be traced back to a process we called TI-2000, when we created a picture of what we wanted our future to be. After carefully studying the long-term outlook for the world electronics industry, relative to our own strengths, our SCG [Semiconductor Group] vision team attempted to answer three questions: (1) Where is the world going?, (2) What will TI's position be?, and (3) How will we get there?[1]

Milliken & Company uses a similar process to align its organization with the environment. For this company, these three basic questions translate into three tasks:

1. Analyze the current situation to understand the internal and external issues that may affect the future success of the organization.
2. Create a compelling management vision that describes the desired future state.
3. Develop a strategy that specifies the action steps needed to achieve the management vision.

These tasks precede all other planning activities in their organization. They help to ensure that external resources continue to flow in a direction that will support the firm. Let's take a look at each of these steps in more detail.

ANALYZE THE CURRENT SITUATION

To establish a frame of reference, many leaders initially define the purpose of their current business. They do this in the form of a mission statement. The mission statement typically answers the questions: *Who are we?* and *What do we do?* In other words, the mission statement articulates the organization's current "reason for being."

The mission statement addresses a number of business variables:

- What business are we in?
- What is our purpose?
- Who are our customers?
- What are the core competencies of our business?
- What are our primary products/services?
- What is our geographic domain?
- What are the key elements of our company philosophy?
- What is our company's self-concept?
- What is our contribution to the quality of life?

A guiding principle, the mission statement lays the groundwork for all mechanistic aspects of a business.

Convert Old 'Scapes Into New Maps

While the mission statement may serve the organization for long periods of time, changes in the environment eventually challenge the organization's fundamental purpose and its core competencies. In other words, you and others in your organization may have adopted certain behaviors, beliefs, and skill sets which led to past success. However, these may be inadequate for meeting today's and tomorrow's challenges. In the words of Kenneth Burke, you may be "fit in an unfit fitness."

Consider a barnyard parable. You can train chickens to interpret the sound of a bell as the signal for food, and then use that same bell to summon them to their death by decapitation. Chickens aren't the only prisoners of their habits.

The parable differentiates two kinds of learning required to succeed in a changing environment. Procedural learning focuses on improving *how* things are done. In the story, the chickens improved familiar procedures to respond faster and faster to the food bell. But sometimes the world changes dramatically, and we need to undo our conventional perceptions of reality. We need to acquire new operational skills to succeed in this changed environment.

To detect critical and/or hidden changes in the environment that require radical change on our part, we must engage in a second type of learning, conceptual learning. This line of inquiry demands an external focus to identify customer murmurs, market issues, societal trends, and other influential dynamics of the system at large. Had the chickens in this story pursued conceptual learning, they might have asked certain questions before naively following the dinner bell. *Why* is the bell sounding? What is the meaning behind the bell? What about our environment has changed?

When we examine the *why* of doing things, not simply the *how*, we can reframe the operational issues in a timely fashion. We can align organizational behavior and skills with critical changes in the environment.

Look Outward and Forward

A situational analysis, conducted periodically, provides one mechanism to see the world in new ways before circumstances force the organization to play catch-up or manage crisis. When we take the time to examine the structural dynamics of our environment, we see how the game must be redefined, the mental models for how to run the business must be modified, and the basic character of the organization transformed.

A situational evaluation requires skills in effective listening, exploring, and building scenarios of alternative futures. Explains Warren Evans of Intel:

> The situation analysis is critical, if nothing more than to validate the vision. At one point in time, our vision was to be at the center of the computer industry. Specifically, our vision was to be the preeminent building block supplier to the computer industry. This vision led us for about five years. Following our situational analysis, we redefined our picture of the future to see the emergence of a new industry, the communications and computer industry. This industry will integrate the cable, wireless, CD, and entertainment industries. It will entail the super-information highway. Today, our vision is to be at the center of this industry. And as new technologies emerge, our strategic vision will change again.

Unfortunately, too many leaders give too little time to evaluating changes in the environment. Gary Hamel and C.K. Prahalad in their *Harvard Business Review* article, "Seeing the Future First," suggest that leaders ask themselves three key questions in this regard. What percentage of your time is spent on external rather than internal issues? Of this time, how much is devoted to envisioning how the world may be different in three to five years? Of the time devoted to looking outward and forward, how much is spent developing a shared vision with other colleagues? Their research indicates that most senior executives spend less than 3% of their time building a corporate perspective of the future!

Observe the System Dynamics

To encourage employees to look outward and forward, many companies rally around slogans like "focus on the customer" and "customer first." But an environmental scan goes beyond customer expectations to include changes in technology, lifestyles, and politics. Anticipating the future requires that we look beyond today's customer to focus on the structural relationships within the wider system and how the organization will prosper in that dynamic environment.

Other companies invest considerable time and money to imagine what this holistic future might look like. Toshiba manages a Lifestyle Research Institute. Sony studies "human science" in parallel with advancements in audiovisual technology. Companies like these focus on answering two questions related to strategic foresight: "What will customers value in tomorrow's products and services?" and "How can our firm deliver these benefits first?"[2] When companies look beyond today's customer satisfaction to generate a holistic description of the future, they enter the world of potential—a firmer grasp of what is really possible.

Use Facts and Analysis to Identify Trends

Companies like Hewlett-Packard and Xerox go to great lengths to analyze changes in their environment (see Figure 1.1, page 48). They use data to identify customer trends, assess the external and internal environment, select improvement opportunities, evaluate progress, and verify corrective action. As a result, their strategic objectives describe realistic ambitions, not mere pipe dreams. Lois Gold describes the data-driven planning process at Hewlett-Packard:

> We use a detailed analytical approach called the ten-step process for developing our three-year plan. It involves a lot of financial and customer analysis. It is not just brainstorming. There are a lot of companies that do not initially have data, so they use brainstorming to get started on a long-term plan. But in our case, we are very data driven. Brainstorming is good in the absence of data, but ultimately you want to drive your management decisions by data, not simply group process techniques.

The Hewlett-Packard ten-step planning process includes a thorough analysis of: (1) the statement of purpose, (2) the five-year objectives, (3) the customer and channels, (4) the competition, (5) necessary products/services, (6) the development/purchase plan, (7) financial indicators, (8) potential problems, and (9) recommendations. This leads to Step 10—develop the plan for the next fiscal year.

Facts inform the planning process. But, in the end, data analysis is not the objective of an environmental scan. Rather, the objective is to reach consensus on the highest points of leverage so as to set priorities for the organization. As John Fly of Milliken warns, "*Data* are facts out of context. *Information* is data interpreted in the context of the way we think about things. *Understanding* is information that defines or changes the way we think about things." When setting direction, the purpose of data analysis is to reframe our perceptions of the environment.

Look for New Themes

A situational analysis can become a complex process of sorting and evaluating ideas, thoughts, opinions, and issues. Customer concerns come in the form of perceptions, demands, and complaints. Employees discuss strengths, weaknesses, opportunities, and threats. They offer observations on system structures that drive the behavior of the firm and its competitors. The volume of these ideas and the ambiguity of language can create confusion and chaos.

This confusion is compounded if we become trapped in our past logic. Comfortable with our past successes, we are not always open to new structures that may be evolving as our environment changes. Old mental models can obscure vital new relationships.

We can simplify the situational analysis when we organize and display language data and then examine our ideas for hidden structural relationships. More subjective than numerical data, language data require a set of special management tools to make key interrelationships visible. (These tools can be found in Appendix B.)

The affinity chart is one such tool. It answers the question, "What are the major issues?" It uses a systematic process to organize issues and concerns in groupings of similar elements to reveal natural relationships and often new relationships. Participants record issues on 3 × 5 cards. Then, they group the cards into common themes. For each category that emerges, a "header card" is written to describe the grouping. The collection of header cards describes the main themes that emerge from the situation analysis. The individual items associated with the headers provide the development details.

There are other methods to enhance the situational analysis. These include the Delphi method (an iterative consensus-building process among experts) and the use of systems thinking, which emphasizes cause-and-effect relationships among system components and feedback relationships that drive behavior.

CREATE A COMPELLING VISION

Once we identify the key issues, we can decide what to do about them. We can position our firm to take advantage of the changing environment.

In setting direction, many managers move directly to create a strategic plan. They believe that, by creating strategic plans, they will ensure a leadership position down the road. However, in the absence of a long-term vision, strategic plans can become an end by themselves rather than a means to achieving a positive higher level purpose. Without the framework of a compelling, informed vision of the desired future state, planning can become a black hole in which the team develops a plan for every possible scenario—a time-consuming and ineffective process.

A vision, simply put, is an objective that lies outside the range of planning. It describes the organization's most desirable future state, and it declares what the organization needs to care about most in order to reach that future state.

Build Unity of Purpose

More than motherhood and apple pie, a management vision extends the mission into the future, inspiring people with diverse skills to work toward a future that is different from today. Consider the traditional management story about the bystander who asked three stone cutters what they were doing. The first replied, "I'm earning my daily wages." The second kept on working while he said: "I am doing the best job of cutting stones in the entire country." The third looked up and declared with enthusiasm: "I am building a cathedral."

Rather than merely cut, polish, and stockpile stones, the third mason understood how his contribution supported the overall enterprise. He likely made appropriate and consistent decisions on the front line. And he probably went beyond the call of duty when problems arose.

A management vision is to today's worker as the cathedral was to the mason in this story. A management vision aligns people with different backgrounds, functional specialties, experiences, and hierarchical positions to channel their unique energies toward the same destination. It relies on a shared mental model to enhance and sustain employee commitment to the change process. And, it utilizes the human capacity for projection. Creating a mental picture of what you want and then holding that expectation unleashes powerful forces that unconsciously move you to take the steps and adopt the attitudes necessary for success.

It is hard to imagine the rise of AT&T, Ford, or Microsoft in the absence of a compelling long-term vision. Theodore Vail envisioned a universal telephone service that took over five decades to achieve. Henry Ford saw ordinary people, not just the privileged, eventually owning cars. William Gates and Paul Allen pursued their vision of "a computer on every desk and in every home." In each case, an individual vision became a shared vision. The vision took the long view. And it described a unique and powerful relationship between the organization and the larger system.

Some leadership teams can easily provide tangible visual details about their desired future state. Yet, this may be more difficult if the industry is changing rapidly. Warren Evans of Intel observes:

> Based on the nature of our industry, it is difficult to have a long-term vision. We do have some ten-year verbiage—this is where we think the world will be—but it is real fuzzy. It is easier to see the next five years.

Even when an organization can not see clearly down the ten-year road, this does not mean that it can't formulate a compelling vision. Consider the management vision of Mystic Valley Regional Medical Center, an organization operating within the turbulent health care industry:

"To be the standard of excellence and cooperation in making Magic Valley the healthiest place in America."

While this vision statement may not provide details, it powerfully links employees, company, community, and nation in a long-term effort. It invites employees to participate in something bigger than any one individual could accomplish on their own.

Get Beyond the Financials

A vision goes beyond financial indicators. Too often, executives define their management vision as "being profitable" or "going public." While "being profitable" is important to staying in business, it does not create a customer. Rather, the purpose of a management vision is to create an "idealized redesign" that will ensure a dominant position in the eye of the customer.

Still other people confuse a vision with a goal. Goals state a specific, measurable step or strategy that can be achieved when you expend effort toward a particular end. Increasing sales by 20%, reducing costs by 10%, and improving quality by 30% are examples of goals. A vision expresses a view of what the future might be, not the how or how much. In the context of a vision, goals and objectives can be verified to be necessary and sufficient.

Many people think that, when developing a management vision, the objective is to "beat the competitor." But when we do nothing more than benchmark others, we limit ourselves to implementing the best of today's known management practices. This can provide valuable industry information, but it generates reactive, not proactive management energy. A compelling vision goes beyond today's competitive arena to identify new opportunities that are "off the current industry map."

Gary Hamel and C.K. Prahalad, in "Seeing the Future First" (*Harvard Business Review*, September/October 1994) state that they prefer the term *foresight* to *vision*. For them, *vision* suggests a dream or fantasy. *Foresight* suggests a deeply informed insight, grounded in profound knowledge of technology and regulatory trends, changing demographics, and lifestyles. Whatever term we use, it is important to differentiate an inspiring set of statements from an informed picture of the future state. Inspiration, alone, can be achieved through advertising, a skill that is grounded primarily in communication. A sound vision must be grounded in evidence of future trends, and it must be robust in the face of alternative future scenarios. The vision must be rational in how it links to the future. Otherwise, people will work at odds with the marketplace.

Create an "Idealized Redesign"

So how can you get beyond the financials? Look at the themes that emerge from the affinity chart and other systems-thinking tools. Start with a blank sheet of paper. Given the current operating environment, design the ideal corporation.

Design elements might include, but are not limited to, organizational structure, products and services, distribution channels, customer service, personnel policies, relationships with regulatory authorities, social and environmental responsibilities, financing, and information and management systems. Again, an affinity chart can be used to organize the various design ideas into a set of vision elements.

The idealized design does not derive from assumptions about the future. Instead, it emerges as a description of the organization that you wish you had today. The most useful new system design:

- openly confronts the current environment,
- is technically feasible,
- is operationally viable,
- is internally consistent, and
- resolves a large number of current problems.

These characteristics should describe the ideal organization to meet today's challenges.[3]

DEVELOP A LONG-TERM STRATEGY: MAP A PATH TO THE FUTURE

Now you have a vision. Beyond a description of market share, profit goals, and revenues, you have created a new organizational concept

The next task is to map the path that will lead you and others to realize this design structure.

There is often a gap between our vision and reality. Peter Senge, in his best selling book on systems thinking, *The Fifth Discipline*, likens this creative tension to a rubber band stretched between the vision and current reality. He warns that tension always seeks resolution or release. So, there are only two possible ways to resolve this tension: the leadership must pull reality toward the vision or it must pull the vision toward reality. The degree to which we *hold steady* to the vision determines our success.[4]

Some people, when faced with this tension, try to reduce the gap by bringing the vision closer to reality. Phrases like "We don't have the resources" or "We do not currently have access to those distribution channels" provide easy excuses for adjusting our vision to fit that which we can do today. But, other leaders view the performance gap as a source of energy. They take ambitious actions to raise reality up to the vision. Rather than focus on what they can do, they focus on what they must do to stretch the organization towards the vision.

This has a lot to do with strategic planning. A strategic plan forms a bridge between the organization's current reason for being and its long-term vision. Specifically, it describes the challenges, opportunities, and priorities for the organization over the next several years. It specifies how the organization will effectively:

- meet changing customer requirements,
- distinguish the organization from its likely competitors, and
- manage internal strengths and weaknesses.

The purpose of the strategic plan is to specify the critical steps in effectively managing an organizational transformation.

Strategic Planning Is a Process, not a Person

A critical first step in designing this plan is, again, to understand the current situation. This includes the system at large and how the organization interacts with that system. A thorough analysis of customers, suppliers, organizational strengths and weaknesses, and environmental variables and their relationships helps to identify the root cause(s) of barriers to achieving the vision. It is critical to understand where the organization is today, where it will remain if it fails to change, and what prevents it from making progress.

Many traditional organizations give this task to a planning department. But, in hoshin management, strategic planning is typically viewed as a process, not a person. It requires the input of a variety of stakeholders including the many employees who work at the boundary of the organization. The executive team, rather than a planning department, takes responsibility for managing this process. John Rogers of Zytec explains:

> The strategic planner role in our company at the strategic thinking level is taken by the cadre of top executives. We have consciously chosen not to have a strategic planner on staff because we think it is *our* responsibility. While I have responsibility for strategic planning, in a hoshin kanri system like ours, it is more of an orchestrating job than an action job. We establish and manage the processes that enable others to contribute and take action. But the output is the result of a lot of different people working together.

As the leadership at Zytec believes, the quality of the strategic plan depends on contributions from a number of different people. When all is said and done, it is not so much the specific details of the plan, but the ability to reach consensus on the current obstacles to progress that creates an informed strategy. This can not be accomplished by assigning the planning task to one person or a single department. Instead, it must involve multiple points of view and multiple stakeholders.

Solicit Multiple Perspectives

John Fly of Milliken observes that "the best strategic visions are created by deeply informed intuitions, especially if they are collective." This requires that the leadership design a planning process that elicits knowledge from as many individuals as possible. Each person holds in his/her head an informed but partial picture of reality.

Again, Zytec, winner of a 1991 Malcolm Baldrige National Quality Award, provides one example of how a participative planning process can help to develop a realistic strategic plan. Even though the company's high-level strategic objective changes slowly over time, the company's planning process uses facts and input from multiple perspectives. To begin the process, the eleven members of the executive team raise questions and suggest strategic issues. Key customer contacts and technology experts assist them in the process.

The myriad of issues are compressed, simplified, and categorized using various planning tools, including affinity diagrams. While the categories emerge naturally throughout the process, they typically describe such areas as markets, technology, manufacturing, materials, corporate policies, and lines of business.

Six to ten senior managers form a team for each category. Approximately half of each team includes area experts. The other half is made up of people from various areas of the company—individuals who can offer a broad cross-functional and hierarchical perspective. Over a period of two months, each team develops a plan for its set of issues, communicating when necessary with the other teams. At the end of the planning period, the teams share their recommendations to identify and resolve disagreements on significant issues.

The Zytec planning documents are succinct. They describe the perceived strategic challenges and summarize benchmarks and action items. Each statement supports the vision by describing the supporting action items for the next two to three years.

Finally, the teams present their plans to the rest of the organization over a period of two days. While attendance is voluntary, Zytec actively encourages employees from all levels of the company to participate. In 1992, about one-fourth of all employees attended a planning session. The leadership aims to eventually get all employees to participate. In recent years, Zytec has included customers and suppliers in addition to the employees.

The two-day planning sessions are managed like a trade show. Each presenting team is assigned a group of 15 attendees. After a summary market analysis and overview of emerging technology, each planning group presents a review of its work. At the conclusions of the presentations, each group of attendees formulates a set of questions and issues pertaining to the presentations. Concerns typically vary from general questions like "Why aren't we developing more new business?" to quite specific questions like "Will population trends in the area of our factory support expected growth?" The planning groups are required to respond to these questions and integrate the resulting insights into their final planning documents. In this way, the employees who are expected to execute the plans are given the opportunity to see the plans in their early stages of formulation and negotiate items. In addition to building commitment, the presentations help each participant interpret the plan for his or her work unit.

At the end of this process, the plans from each group are combined to develop a financial projection of the entire strategic plan. In other words, Zytec manages the financial plan as a condition-testing event. The plans must produce numbers that support the company's mission. Observes John Rogers of Zytec,

> Traditionally, strategic planning uses a lot of market data and financial data. But, in the hoshin kanri approach, there is a lot of actual operating data like quality levels, turnaround times and warehouse loading factors. This is a considerable difference. Hoshin kanri is a detailed execution-oriented process, whereas strategic planning, as normally conceived, is pretty broad based. In the hoshin kanri context, you view the financial statements, not as a beginning point; e.g. "We have to get a return of such and such to be acceptable in the market place." But rather, we view the financial statement as an end point; e.g. "When we did all this stuff, we got a return on investment of such and such." In hoshin kanri, it is an output, not an input; it is an indicator of how successful our strategies are.

In other words, Zytec uses the data to inform the planning process, not just as a set of financial indicators.

Long-term and intermediate plans derive from a careful assessment of several variables:

- customers
- the environment
- the vision
- the current situation
- past performance
- employee concerns
- senior management concerns

These and other issues influence the strategic imperatives identified during the strategic planning process.

Use Reverse Design Principles to Map a Path from Today to the Future

Many people, when confronted with the planning task, look for comfortable, predictable, and conservative steps forward. They create a plan in a "10-year, 10% per year" linear, step-by-step fashion. But, these traditional planning methodologies fail to provide the behavioral guidance that an organization needs to achieve its vision. They fail to describe *how* the organization must change each year to achieve those goals.

An alternative approach to planning is variously called "idealized redesign," "backward planning," or "ends planning." Initially described by Russell Ackoff in his book, *Creating the Corporate Future*, this creative process starts with a picture of the ideal organization for today's environment and backward derives the current state of affairs. In other words, the planning process takes place in reverse fashion.

Starting with the ideal design, managers iteratively apply constraints on that system until they arrive at the current design. Working backwards, year by year, they identify as many constraints as they can eliminate in one year. The outcome of this planning process is a map for undoing the current system in a way that generates the ideal design.

Russell Ackoff's creative process gives leaders a systematic rather than anecdotal approach to innovative redesign. It avoids straight linear predictions of change, an inappropriate approach to innovation and achieving dramatic improvements in performance. It generates *breakthrough* strategies as opposed to the more conventional approaches using old mental models. The plan is usually shorter than the typical ten-year plan that emerges from more traditional linear strategic planning methodologies.

SUMMING IT UP

In the end, a management mission, vision, and strategy are not simply clever things to have; they are *active* tools of management. They are the ultimate responsibility of senior management and form the basis of strategic intent. While organization-wide consensus is needed to create a shared purpose, top management is responsible for shaping and effectively communicating the strategic intent. Clear direction helps to mobilize and coordinate activity throughout the organization.

Yet, certain questions remain. Once the leadership sets the direction, how can it translate its vision and long-term strategies into dramatic, measurable outcomes? How can the leadership guarantee that employees will focus on those opportunities that offer the great-

Figure 1.1. Clarify the vision.

Situation Analysis: View of the World

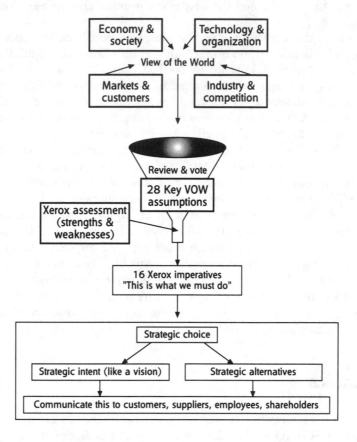

Source: Xerox Corporation. Used by permission.

est advantage? This leads us to the next chapter where we will see how some companies convert the generalities of their vision into a specific set of measurable objectives that the organization can understand and act upon.

NOTES

1. Pat Weber, "Management View, TQC: Five Years later, Why It Was the Right Formula for Unlocking SCG's Potential," *TQC World*, June 1994, p. 18.

2. Gary Hamel and C.K. Prahalad, "Strategic Intent," *Harvard Business Review*, May/June, p. 66.
3. Russell L. Acknoff, *Creating the Corporate Future—Plan or Be Planned for* (New York: Wiley & Sons, 1981).
4. Peter M. Senge, *The Fifth Discipline: The Art and Practice of the Learning Organization* (New York: Doubleday/Currency, 1990), pp. 150.

2

Sharpen the Focus:
Select the Vital Few Breakthrough Objectives

*Strategic intent is like a marathon run in 400-meter sprints.
No one knows what the terrain will look like at mile 26, so
the role of top management is to focus the organization's
attention on the ground to be covered in the next 400
meters.* —Gary Hamel and C.K. Prahalad

A chairman and CEO of a regional bank recently declared, "Number two is not good enough for me! I want to be number one in the eyes of the customer. I want to put this bank on the map as a world class financial services institution!"

Today, there is hardly a single CEO who does not declare in the most convincing way, with moist eyes and fist in the air, that he or she wants to be number one. Yet despite "customer first," process reengineering, employee empowerment, and other programs of the day, three out of four organizations fail to achieve their strategic intent.

Today, leaders need more than inspiration and haphazard attempts to achieve their visions and long-term strategies. They need to identify and communicate the vital few competencies that will catapult the organization toward its vision. The clearer the priorities are, the easier it is for employees to focus on what really counts and to take action.

SET PRIORITIES TO ALIGN EMPLOYEES

Such a focused approach to change has a lot to do with hoshin management. In hoshin management, the leaders identify the critical few strategies that support the long-term vision, specify the key systems that need to be improved to achieve these objectives, and then clearly communicate that agenda throughout the organization. They specify the vital few priorities requiring collective action over the next months, often up to a year.

Called "hoshins," these annual priorities translate the strategic vision into operational requirements. Whereas a vision states, "This is where we are going," hoshins state, "These are the critical few performance gaps that we must close today to achieve our vision." Hoshins constantly remind people of what the organization is trying to change. If the strategic plan is the map, then hoshins specify the route, or means, that the organization will take in its next fiscal year to achieve its destination.

"Well," you might be thinking, "we already establish annual objectives. What is so different here?" One answer is linkage. In hoshin management, every annual objective derives from the long-term plan. In MBO, corporate goals frequently become detached from the strategic plan. Employees are unable to see any connection between annual goals and the strategic picture, especially if the goals are expressed in financial terms. But in hoshin management, every annual objective is linked to the long-term strategy. And every employee can see the logic. Observes Dorothy Bellhouse of Sewickley Hospital:

> Before we adopted the hoshin management system, our planning system was not integrated. The strategic plan set the tone only. It was not directly linked to the budget or to the development of annual objectives. Our annual budget was essentially a stand-alone process and financially driven. Annual objectives were developed after we completed the budget. They were not tied to our prior year's performance. And there was no direct linkage to our strategic plan. With hoshin management, our annual objectives are now seen as part of the total planning process and are developed before the budget. Our strategic plan includes six imperatives and all annual objectives are designed to move forward toward one or more of these.

Annual objectives can either work toward the vision or confound the process. Linking annual objectives with the strategic intent brings focus and control to the change process.

This chapter looks at how the hoshin planning process achieves that linkage.

Two Types of Activity Work Toward the Vision

In any given year, there are many opportunities to advance toward the vision. While all contributions are welcome, the purpose of the hoshin management system is to select those annual objectives that will give the organization the greatest possible advantage.

To this end, hoshin management recognizes and distinguishes two kinds of annual contributions:

1. incremental improvements to existing processes or methods ("kaizen"), and
2. activities aimed at making dramatic improvements in strategically vital business systems and processes ("hoshin").

A plan to achieve the vision must include both sets of activities. (See Figure 2.1.)

Incremental, non-breakthrough activities improve the health of key business processes. Employees, often working in teams, use facts and analysis to solve recurring problems. They use the scientific methods to standardize and improve existing processes—the SDCA (Standardize-Do-Check-Act) and PDSA (Plan-Do-Study-Act) cycles for continuous improvement. These activities and the management tools that support them are typically associated with the school of total quality management, describe reactive improvement, and are captured by the word "kaizen."

However, some performance gaps are large and cannot be closed using an incremental approach to improvement. A 5% improvement may be achieved by adjusting existing business systems, but a dramatic improvement in performance often requires greater change:

- an entirely new process or a radical departure from an existing one,
- a new pattern of resource allocation,
- coordinated effort by more than one department of the organization, or
- concentrated effort over an extended period of time, often more than one year.

Figure 2.1. Breakthrough strategies change the way we do business.

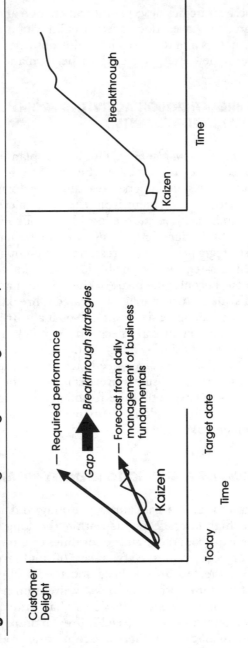

Because these strategies describe radical change and are strategically so significant, they are often called breakthrough strategies. Breakthrough strategies aim to overcome major obstacles or systemic problems to achieve new levels of growth or performance.

SEPARATE BREAKTHROUGH ACTIVITIES FROM INCREMENTAL IMPROVEMENTS

This is the focus of hoshin planning. The hoshin planning system identifies and concentrates resources on the vital few *stretch* achievements that support the vision. It separates those performance issues that require dramatic improvement from the many incremental improvements that can be achieved at the local level. (See Figure 2.2.) All the changes that the leadership believes to be incremental are skimmed out of the strategic plan and addressed through quality in daily work. The remaining category of contribution—the vital few breakthrough achievements—becomes the heart of the hoshin management system.

Does this mean that managing strategic breakthroughs is more important than managing daily work? Not at all! Breakthrough activities and daily maintenance are necessary parallel processes to ensure the health of the business. They both need to be managed in a disciplined way. Each manager needs to ensure that the basic processes that support the business are healthy. At the same time, each manager needs to ensure that the fundamental changes and competencies necessary for the long-term health of the organization are being implemented.

USE BACKWARDS PLANNING TO IDENTIFY BREAKTHROUGHS

Hoshin planning uses a backwards planning and linkage system to identify the high-leverage points within the long-term strategy. It works backwards from the vague generalities of the vision to articulate long-term objectives, to specify a set of mid-term breakthrough achievements, then to isolate those short-term objectives that offer the greatest promise within the next twelve months. The result is a set of annual or six-month objectives that dramatically move the organization toward its vision (see Figure 2.5 on page 59).

In hoshin management, there are four basic levels of abstraction:

Figure 2.2. The hoshin planning process distinguishes breakthroughs from incremental improvements.

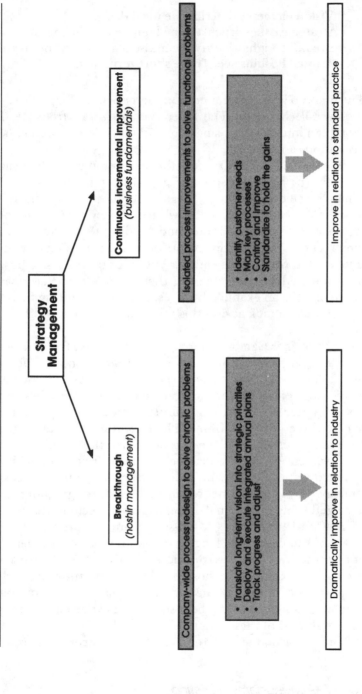

- Vision elements describe the ideal design.
- Strategic issues articulate the long-term challenges.
- Breakthroughs identify the mid-term "stretch" opportunities.
- Annual hoshins specify the short-term tasks.

The first two levels of stratification (described in Chapter 1) formulate the overall challenge. The latter two categories translate the long-term plan into practical language and tangible requirements that the institution can act upon.

At every level of abstraction, the leadership uses a filtering system to select the vital few strategic gaps that must be closed. When it comes to achieving strategic breakthroughs, it is not sufficient merely to select targets. "Vital" and "few" are two key concepts in mobilizing members of the organization and holding their attention. Because the process forces selection, contributions are pragmatic and concentrate on the foreseeable future. The filtering process tends to compress and reduce ideas, making them concrete and actionable. (See Figure 2.3 for an example from a small manufacturing firm.)

Let's take a look at how this works at a number of different companies.

At Procter & Gamble, annual objectives derive from the long-term strategic plan, which looks out over ten years or more. The long-term plan is "indexed down" to more specific strategies with five-year goals. These mid-term goals are used to select what P&G calls "important areas." These are areas that will demand special attention within a one- to three-year time frame. The important areas are subsequently analyzed to establish which business variables require the greatest improvement or might which be the most difficult to achieve. From this analysis, the leadership finally selects the annual breakthrough strategy. Any key areas not requiring breakthrough improvement are managed using quality in daily management techniques.

Hewlett-Packard uses a ten-step planning process described in Chapter 1 to convert its long-term plan into action. It identifies a set of three- to five-year breakthrough objectives. (See Figure 2.4.) Then it creates an annual, or hoshin, plan for the next fiscal year that supports and links with the long-term plan. If the environment is changing rapidly, this can be a six-month cycle. Figure 2.5 presents an overall view of these relationships.

The Semiconductor Group at Texas Instruments uses a four-

Figure 2.3. Filter the opportunities.

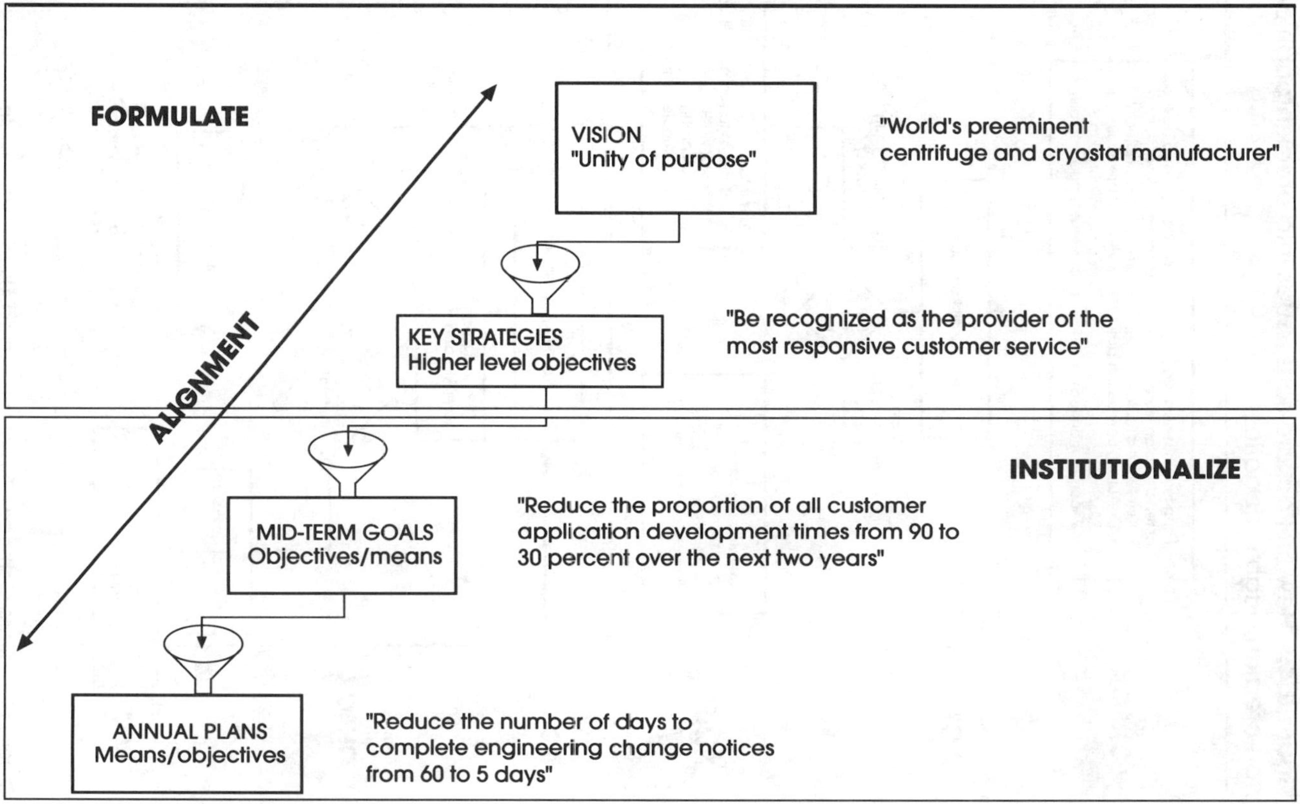

FORMULATE

INSTITUTIONALIZE

ALIGNMENT

VISION
"Unity of purpose"

"World's preeminent centrifuge and cryostat manufacturer"

KEY STRATEGIES
Higher level objectives

"Be recognized as the provider of the most responsive customer service"

MID-TERM GOALS
Objectives/means

"Reduce the proportion of all customer application development times from 90 to 30 percent over the next two years"

ANNUAL PLANS
Means/objectives

"Reduce the number of days to complete engineering change notices from 60 to 5 days"

Figure 2.4. Hewlett-Packard sorts issues into breakthrough and non-breakthrough categories.

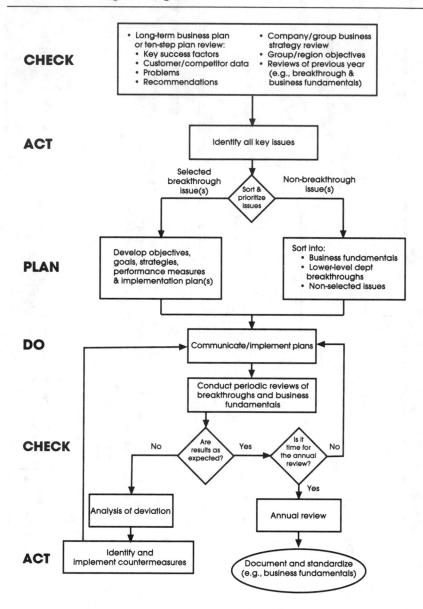

Figure 2.5. Translate the generalizations of the long-term plan into measurable short-term objectives.

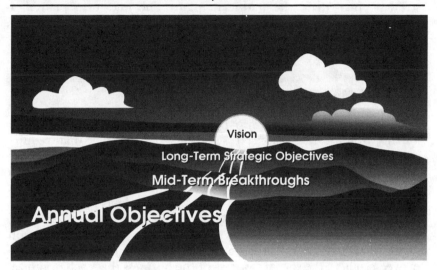

step process to translate their strategic intent into annual priorities. Explains Ron McCormick:

> We started with the TI vision, which describes what we want to be as a company. We want to be a leading worldwide semi-conductor company achieving customer satisfaction, serving worldwide customers, and shifting more of our product mix from what we had been known for in the past, which was standard products, to differentiated products.
>
> Our next step was to select the key priorities that the management wanted to focus the organization on for the next three to five years. For us, these priorities include: customer number one, excellence in everything we do, worldwide and market driven strategies leading to model profitability, and increased market share. We believe that if we do well on these priorities in the next to three to five years, then we will be well on the way to realizing our long-term vision.
>
> For each priority, we then selected performance measures to track progress and set stretch goals. For instance, "Customer number one" is a great slogan. But we need to know how well we are doing at satisfying customers. So, we selected customer satisfaction surveys, on-time deliveries, product defect levels, and customer disruptions. For each of these indicators, the company then set excellence goals for three to five years out as well as annual goals.

Regardless of the specific approach, hoshin management is a process of focusing and aligning. The mission, vision, and long-term strategic plan drive the mid-term plan. The mid-term plan then drives the annual or short-term hoshin plan. The short-term plan drives the implementation or tactical action plans. *All objectives are measurable.*

DESIGN A MID-TERM PLAN

The purpose of the mid-term plan is to map a three- to five-year journey toward the vision. It separates those issues that require dramatic change from the many incremental improvements that can be achieved through daily work. A critical part of the management team's job is to prioritize work and concentrate on those issues that have the greatest impact on the delivery of products and services to the customer. The mid-term plan documents their choices.

While company visions may share generic characteristics with other organizations (such as improved customer satisfaction or improved quality), the specific aspects of the business that each organization wants to change are likely to vary. The breakthroughs specify what, precisely, the senior leadership wishes to change in the next several years, and communicates these priorities in a practical format. In other words, the breakthrough strategies reflect senior managers' interpretation of the vital few success factors and core competencies needed for innovation and market success.

Every hoshin management company customizes its planning process. However, a sequential set of questions guides the development of the mid-term plan:

- Where *could* we improve?
- Where *should* we focus?
- Where *must* we focus?
- Where *will* we intervene?

The answers to these questions generate the mid-term objectives.

Identify Improvement Opportunities

Where could we improve? The first step in the mid-term planning process is to create an *exhaustive* list of improvement opportunities. These opportunities emerge from

- a review of the long-term plan, and
- a situation analysis, which brings short-term reality to the long-term objectives.

While it may seem redundant, the situation analysis at this stage of the planning process is not to be confused with the one described in Chapter 1. The purpose of the situation analysis in Chapter 1 is to shape the vision. The situation analysis at this stage of the planning process integrates any customer, competitive, environmental, or other issues that impede the organization from making progress toward its vision. The outcome is a set of mid-term challenges.

There are many ways to conduct a situation analysis. Many companies, however, start at the bottom and go through each business unit, section, or organizational level until the key issues are identified. Most companies combine information about customers, current challenges, and the long-term challenges. Situational variables include:

- customer needs
- past performance data
- employee concerns
- industry trends
- competitive benchmarks
- top management concerns
- vision elements and long-term strategy

To add rigor to the situation analysis, employees use data analysis and planning tools to collect and display the data, and to justify and compare the issues. These include, but are not limited to, the fishbone diagram, affinity diagram, interrelationship digraph, and the Pareto chart.

Zytec makes this a participative process. Through a series of group forums, employees and managers study the situation to identify the obstacles and opportunities. The intention is not simply to generate good ideas; it is to identify specific measurable opportunities.

Participants bring a set of external and internal issues with a portfolio of supporting data (benchmarks, in particular). For example, the operations department head will contribute issues and data related to operations. The marketing person will bring marketing issues and data. The focus is on the question, "What do we need to worry about?" If, for example, the issue is "time to market," then it is presented as "We lag our competitors by six months; here are the data to support my position."

From the combined material, the participants brainstorm improvement opportunities and display these ideas randomly on cards. They use an affinity diagram to identify common themes among the opportunities. The outcome of this planning step is a list of the key issues and challenges facing the organization in the mid-term. These may be such general success factors as industry trends, customer service, and emerging technologies. But they eventually lend themselves to measurement—a valuable tool, as we will see later in the planning process.

At Procter & Gamble, the process of generating improvement opportunities also leads to measurements. Observes David Lord:

> We call them critical measures. I wish we had done these first. I think it is important that the organization be real clear about what are the important measures for the organization. Probably 90% of them have been the same for many years—cost, customer service items, organizational capability measures. Yet there is a tremendous amount of variation in these. What we found is that these critical processes differ by industry.

By positioning the critical issues first, leaders can focus the subsequent improvement activities.

Identify the Breakthroughs

Where should we focus? A thorough situational analysis generates a myriad of improvement opportunities. The next step is to separate the *breakthroughs* from the incremental opportunities. Lois Gold observes:

> Each year we go through the process of prioritizing. At any point in time, there are always more things that we can work on than we have the resources for. What hoshin planning does is force us to discipline. The planning process is not a wish list of all the things we should address this year—instead it picks out the one or two or three priorities that we are really going to put together with detailed plans to make sure that they happen. We will address some of the other issues if we have resources left over. Some issues are just going to be left on the table, because they cannot all get addressed by the organization.

The challenge is to identify the largest strategic gaps, even if they seem impossible to close. Observes Wayne Bernetti, former vice president of Florida Power & Light:

Many people think that targets must be achievable. This is utter nonsense. Every time I hear that phrase it says to me that targets should be easy to achieve. Targets must stretch the organization's ability and capability to get it accomplished. If you don't, your competitors will.

Often executives love stretch objectives. They initially imagine breakthroughs to "be profitable" or "go public." While being profitable is important to staying in business, and may indeed require a management breakthrough, such an objective does not create a customer. The purpose of a hoshin breakthrough is to focus the organization on a strategic challenge that will ensure a dominant position in the eye of the customer. The trick is to get beyond the financial expectations to specify the operational requirements.

Other people pick stretch objectives that describe changes in the culture, like "increase employee motivation" or "increase employee morale." Such objectives are actually the means to achieve something bigger. The most useful stretch objectives describe an operational challenge to deliver a customer-focused benefit.

A small set of criteria can help ensure that employees identify operational breakthroughs. Does this opportunity:

- Provide a significant benefit to the customer?
- Change the basis of competition?
- Describe an operational challenge?
- Derive from facts and analysis?
- Require a radically new allocation of resources?
- Appear to be "undoable"?
- Create a new standard and/or system?

One popular management tool that filters options and evaluates the alternatives is a two-dimensional matrix diagram. Sometimes called the "critical issue decision matrix" or the "prioritization matrix," this tool visually displays the relationships between a set of candidates and a set of selection criteria. (See Figure 2.6.) The options are placed in horizontal rows. The criteria by which they will be evaluated are placed in vertical columns. Visual symbols at the intersections indicate the strength of the relationship.

The nature and weights of the selection criteria differ by company, organization within the company, and by the stage of consolidation. But, in general, teams array the options using criteria such as

Figure 2.6. Use a prioritizion matrix to identify breakthroughs.

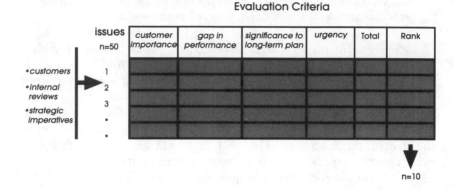

importance to the customer, urgency, size of performance gap, and degree of organization-wide commitment needed to succeed. The issues that emerge with the highest scores become the short list of candidates for intervention.

The outcome of this step is a list of breakthrough issues facing the organization. All of the non-breakthrough items are handed over to functional groups as possible pursuits, or set aside completely.

Conduct a Gap Analysis

Where must we focus? Due to limited resources, companies that practice hoshin management filter the long list of breakthrough opportunities to identify the *most promising candidates* for company-wide attention. They reduce the number of "should do" items to the vital few actions that it "must do."

To help pare the list down, some companies assign an indicator to measure the gap and then conduct a gap analysis for each break-through candidate. The purpose of the gap analysis is to integrate strategic direction with operational knowledge. For this reason, the people who know the most about these issues help to refine the analysis. Some of the breakthrough issues may be functional issues; others may be cross-functional in scope. The nature of the break-through dictates the appropriate research team.

Making choices can be difficult. John Hudiburg, former chairman of the board and CEO of Florida Power & Light, winner of the prestigious Deming Prize awarded in Japan for total quality perform-ance, emphasizes the importance of making those hard decisions in his book, *Winning with Quality*:

> One of our early mistakes in policy management was a common one: we tried to work on too many things at once. The first time we went through the process, if someone suggested dropping an item from the quality element (customer requirements) list, they were looked at as if they were proposing murder. Our counselor's way of putting it was that we were chasing too many rabbits at the same time. Eventually we narrowed down the number of things designated for major improvements to just the vital few . . . There were only eight elements on the list for the entire organization . . . Moreover, any given department would only work on about three of these at the same time (pp. 45–46).

As Hudiburg and his team learned, one key step to harnessing corporate energy is to select two or three "vital few" strategies upon which to focus. The team chooses indicators to measure each gap. They evaluate how much each breakthrough contributes to the larger performance gaps. Then they determine the required resources. The goal is to understand just what impact each candidate will contribute to the long-term objectives.

There are many techniques to identify the vital few strategic gaps. However, many companies use Pareto analysis and root cause analysis to identify the high leverage points within their long-term strategic objectives.

To complete the analysis, the team brainstorms the sequence of activities needed to achieve each breakthrough. A tree diagram can be used to identify gaps in logic, translate general needs into operational requirements, and map all possible means, departments, and tasks over a multi-year period.

The outcome of this step is a short list of candidates for break-through strategies. Each one is presented in the form of a refined problem statement and a proposed sequence of annual tasks. Whereas the initial list of candidates for stretch objectives might be as many as 50, the short list may be closer to ten. The remaining 40 issues are relegated to daily management, if they are pursued at all.

Select the Vital Few Breakthroughs

Where will we intervene? From the short list of breakthrough candi-dates, the executive team selects *one to three* mid-term objectives. Using additional matrix analysis and several of the other planning tools, the team documents its logic. Again, the remaining breakthroughs are relegated to daily management.

Breakthrough opportunities are often interrelated. Making inroads in one direction may have an indirect impact on one or more critical breakthroughs. The challenge is to identify those breakthroughs which will make the most dramatic improvements toward the vision. Leaders often choose to work first on those success factors that significantly influence others.

An interrelationship diagraph of the breakthrough candidates can add some causal insight. By identifying the high leverage points, or most promising interventions, it can help set priorities. The interrelationship diagraph answers the question: Which factor causes or influences another? Using one way arrows, participants map the causal relationships among the issues. Then they identify which breakthrough(s) drives the system of interrelated issues. The "driver" (generally identified by the largest net number of outbound arrows) is a good place to start to positively impact the surrounding environment. (See Figure 2.7.) This process often highlights the "root cause" barriers to progress in an interacting system of success factors.

What does this filtering process actually look like? At one large high-tech firm in Boston, participants generated over 800 opportunities during their situational analysis. Employee teams subsequently reduced this list to 50 breakthroughs. Using affinity diagrams, structure trees, and matrices, they organized and displayed these diverse opportunities. They used an interrelationship diagraph to examine the logical, not merely inductive dynamics among their opportunities. They combined their issues even further to create a short list of ten breakthroughs. For each breakthrough candidate, the teams next created problem statements and used a matrix with criteria that ranked the opportunities. They collected more data, and used Pareto analysis to isolate problem components and to generate countermeasures. The employee team presented the final set of breakthrough candidates to the management team who used additional matrix analysis and criteria to select what they believed to be the vital three measurable mid-term breakthrough priorities for the organization.

Texas Instruments uses a similar process. The leadership selected four mid-term breakthrough priorities and assigned indicators and

Figure 2.7. Use an interrelationship diagraph to map the systems dynamics.

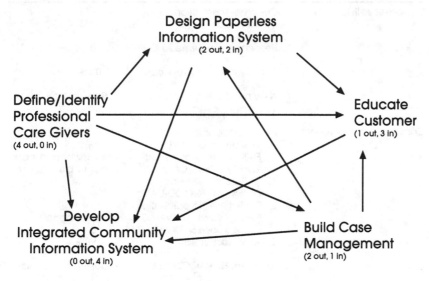

Source: Parkview Episcopal Medical Center. Used by permission.

stretch goals to track progress. (See Figure 2.8.) Observes Ron McCormick of Texas Instruments:

> The purpose of this process is to get results. So, the key metrics must be well communicated and understood. If you are a worldwide company, or a very large company, you must work especially hard to create consistent definitions across all organizations. That way, when you track the strategic gaps and their indices, every region is tracking them the same way.

Whatever the process, whatever the tools, the intent of this stage of the mid-term plan is three-fold:

1. Identify one to three breakthrough objectives requiring multi-year effort on the part of the organization. These breakthrough objectives describe management's interpretation of the critical success factors in achieving the vision.
2. Determine the preliminary responsibilities and annual sequencing of key tasks to achieve these objectives.

Figure 2.8. Describe mid-term breakthroughs in measurable terms.

Priorities	Performance measures	Excellence goals
Customer satisfaction	1. Customer satisfaction surveys (% satisfied)	# 1 Rank
	2. Percent not on time to CD	0
	3. Quality returns % revenue	0.1%
	4. New products on time Percent on-time	90%
Continuous improvement	5. Mfg excellence	
	A. FAB process yield	98%
	B. FAB cost improvement (FAB$/GOOD-CM2)	Industry benchmark Industry benchmark
	C. FAB asset efficiency ($NFA+WIP/GOOD-CM2)	
	D. Cycle time (95 percentile) Percent flows <6 XVAThCT Percent flows >7 XVAThCT	Industry benchmark 0
	E. Assy/ test yield	98%
	6. Net revenue/GOOD CM2	Industry benchmark
	7. Profitability RONA%	25%
	8. Market share Total market penetration WSTS DSP market penetration	Market leader Market leader
People involvement	9. Training Percent linear to meet goal	70 Hrs/person

Source: Texas Instruments. Used by permission.

3. Achieve consensus on the items not selected as breakthrough priorities and assigned to daily management.

With the mid-term plan, the leverage is in going from an independent activity-based approach to performance improvement to a company-wide effort which is driven by a few critical priorities.

SELECT THE ANNUAL HOSHINS

Mid-term breakthrough objectives specify the critical few performance gaps that must be closed within three to five years to ensure a strategic position. Yet, employees still need to know what they can do *today* to support the effort, which aspects of the status quo they must change *first* in the multi-year effort.

Few managers have the capability to focus on more than three "major impact" or "vital few" items at a time. For this reason, annual objectives or "hoshins" are few in number—two or three at most per year.

Hoshins bring focus, specificity, and measurability to the mid-term plan. Whereas five-year or mid-term objectives link the vision to where the organization is today, a hoshin specifies precisely which competencies employees must focus on in the next twelve months to make dramatic inroads toward the five-year objectives.

Three sequential questions guide the development of the annual objectives:

- What *could* we do to intervene?
- What *should* we do to intervene?
- What *will* we do to intervene?

The team uses many of the same tools and techniques that they used earlier to select the mid-term breakthrough objectives. They conduct a gap analysis of each mid-term breakthrough issue to identify the root cause obstructions to improved performance and develop a set of means or competencies to close the gaps. Then they compare alternatives to identify the highest leverage points within the mid-term strategy. Finally, the executive team selects the vital few measurable priorities for the fiscal year. All other items are again addressed through daily management, if at all.

Identify all Possible Means to Close the Gap

What could we do to intervene? To begin the annual planning process, the executive team invites its direct reports to join them in the development of the annual hoshin objectives. The subordinates are responsible for developing the proposed annual hoshins and presenting them back to management for final selection.

Based on its earlier analysis during the mid-term planning phase, the executive team initially suggests the means to close each strategic gap. They offer ideas based upon analysis, experience, management direction, or a combination of all three. Then they invite their subordinates to review and critique their sequencing of activities. The intent is to give the next level of management a starting point, *not* a directive.

The subordinates, who are closer to the realities of the business, can now brainstorm a list of "to do's" that will generate a positive impact on the drivers identified in the mid-term plan. Observes Lois Gold from Hewlett-Packard:

> Key questions include: What are the things that we potentially need to work on this year to move us toward accomplishing our five-year plan and the long-term vision? What are the customer satisfaction issues that we are seeing at our level? Are there any objectives that we didn't complete last year that are still a priority? We put together a basket of potential issues each fiscal year.

Subordinates use situation analysis and a root cause problem solving process to explore the gap between current performance and each of the mid-term goals. Then they conduct a situational analysis to ensure the appropriateness of their strategies. The situational analysis at this stage of the planning process integrates customer input, operational challenges, and other environmental issues affecting the next planning cycle. They study the resource requirements of each hoshin candidate. The outcome is a set of recommended solutions, resource requirements, and an estimate of how much each solution will contribute to closing the gap.

Identify High Impact Methods

What should we do to intervene? A systematic review of all the opportunities can verify the appropriateness of the proposed solutions. Gold notes:

> Out of the bucket of issues, you have to prioritize which ones you are going to pick off to address in that fiscal year. You look at the issues against the five-year objectives to see where you might get multiple impact. You can use criteria like urgency, etc., but also how they impact the five-year objectives, looking for where we can kill two birds with one stone.

Employees assess each proposed hoshin to ensure that it will indeed:

- change the basis of competition.
- have organizational importance.
- require a year-long effort.
- describe a change in operations.
- be able to be measured.

Regardless of the company criteria, participants filter the many opportunities to identify the few that are critical to success. To this end, it can be helpful to answer the questions: "What if we select this opportunity?" and "What if we don't?"

Some companies use a matrix diagram called the "T matrix" to evaluate the alternatives. This matrix compares the set of possible interventions with the key business systems or processes and the key customer demands. The means to positively impact the breakthroughs are listed across the middle of the matrix. The key business process is spread out on the upper left hand side of the matrix. The degree of impact that any one opportunity has on customer demands and internal processes is identified with a visual symbol and may be weighted with a 9 = high, 3 = medium, and 1 = low system. The activities with the greatest impact across the internal and external system are the hoshins. (See Figure 2.9.)

Upon completing this step, teams present the executive team with a list of candidates for the annual hoshins and their rationale. They recommend measures and countermeasures. The intention is to share knowledge, increase clarity, and build consensus on the selection process.

Select One to Three Annual Objectives

What will we do to intervene? There are always more opportunities than an organization can ever do in one year. So, the executive team must filter and select the most promising set of one to three annual objectives, prior to budgeting.

The emphasis at this stage of the planning process is on synergy. The executive team must select the optimum mix of hoshins. Whatever the selection of the specified competencies, they must be sufficient to achieve the mid-term plan. All other items are relegated to daily management.

Often, the hardest part of selecting hoshins is to accept and live with the choices you make. A decision to focus on one or two aspects

Figure 2.9. A T-Matrix.

Pre-Admission Hoshin

	Patient	Physician	Patient	Physician	Patient	Physician	Patient	Physician	Patient	Physician	Patient	Physician
Need for Service	◐	○	●	●	●	○	n/a	n/a	●	●	●	○
3rd Party Payor Data	●	◐	○	○	◐	○	n/a	n/a	●	◐	●	○
Coordinate Arrival		●		n/a		●		n/a		n/a		
MR Access	◐	◐	●	◐	○	◐	n/a	n/a	◐	○	●	○
Case Management Research Begins (URN)	○	●	○	●	○	●	○	●	●	●	●	
Pre-Hospital Case Management Begins	◐	●	○	●	○	●	●	◐	●	●	●	
Pre-Hospital Case Management Integrated Internal	◐	◐	n/a	n/a	n/a	n/a	◐	●	●	●	●	

Key Business Strategies ↑ Customer Expectations ↓	Patient Demographics		Prior Knowledges		Access Clinical Info		Access Psycho-Social Info		Wellness		Evaluation Format	
Efficiency	○	●	○	◐	●	●	○	●	●	●	●	○
Accuracy	●	●	◐	●	●	●	◐	●	●	●	●	
Completeness	●	◐	◐	●	●	●	●	●	●	●	●	
One Stop Visit	○	●	○	●	○	●	○	●	n/a	n/a	○	
No Repeat Information	○	●	○	●	○	●	○	●	n/a	n/a	○	
Patient Expected	○	○	○	●	○	●	○	●	n/a	n/a	○	
Prepared for Patient's Family	○	●	○	●	○			○	n/a		◐	
Informed	n/a	n/a	n/a	n/a	◐	◐	◐	◐	●	●	◐	
Easy Access	n/a	n/a	n/a	n/a	n/a	n/a	n/a	n/a	n/a	n/a	○	
Access PEMC Database	●	○	●	●	●	●	●	◐	●	◐	●	○
Personalized Attention	○	●	○	●	◐	●	◐	●	○	●	○	
	99	55	106	42	107	61	84	39	88	94	123	101

● = 9 ◐ = 3 ○ = 1

Source: Parkview Hospital. Used by permission.

of your business is also a decision to give up other opportunities. But focus is key to managing change. While it is tempting to want to work on a large number of items, it is the leader's ability to set priorities that enables the organization to succeed.

Once the management team selects one to three annual hoshins, the job is not complete. The mid-term planning process and the selection of the annual hoshins is an iterative process. When the executive team selects the final set of annual hoshins, it goes back to modify the mid-term plan to reflect these choices. In this way, the annual plan and the mid-term plan link to create a dynamic rolling plan.

THE NATURE OF A HOSHIN

When all is said and done, what exactly does a hoshin look like? It differs by company. Some organizations select high level targets like "reduce late shipments." Other companies select means like "reduce cycle time." Still others select a target with a mean such as "increase customer satisfaction by reducing cycle time." Whatever the format, annual hoshin objectives are customer focused, deeply informed, behavioral, and measurable. Rather than announce an annual objective like "increase sales by 15%," the hoshin planning process specifies the critical few competencies by which the leadership hopes this will happen. (See Figure 2.10 for an "X-matrix" used by a small manufacturing firm to clarify relationships among mid-term objectives, annual priorities, and measures to close the strategic gaps.)

Intel's model for picking measurable hoshins includes three areas of focus. Typically, one hoshin focuses on the needs of the current customers and product concerns. The second hoshin emphasizes new product development issues in a changing environment. The third hoshin describes an internal breakthrough objective, e.g., upgrading the people, processes, and systems. They filter their improvement activities into these three buckets.

The Semiconductor Group at Texas Instruments numerically links its annual stretch targets with its five-year goals. For example, one of its five-year objectives is to "increase customer satisfaction." One indicator selected to measure this objective, identified through customer feedback, is to "reduce late shipments." The goal associated with this indicator is "zero." The first-year goal was to bring late

Figure 2.10. Specify the strategies and measures to close the strategic gaps.

	Improve external quality rate as measured by units returned on warranty vs. total units shipped	Reduce internal reject rate as measured by scrap and rework $	Improve on-time delivery as measured by % time filled to customer request code specified on sales order	Expand sales base of new products as measured by total new product $ sales	Management of new product introductions	
Improve operating income to XX%						
Provide "World Class" quality						
Provide "World Class" customer service						
Improve sales growth to XX%						
Reduce warranty cost % of units returned by X% from ____ to ____.	O					
Reduce scrap & rework as a % of costs by Y% from ____ to ____.		O				
Improve first-pass quality acceptance rate from X% to Y%.		O O				
Improve order entry accuracy from X% to Y%.		O				
Improve delivery from X% to Y% on time to customer request date by ____			O			
Reduce all product lead times to less than 2 weeks by ____.			O			
New product A sales to $X.				O		
New product B sales to $X.				O O		
New product C sales to $X for OEM custom applications.				O		
On-time performance and cost targets					O	
Operations	●	●	●	O	O	
Sales and marketing			O	●	●	
Finance						
Human resources						
Research and development				O	●	
General manager		O	O	O	O	

Benefits · 3-5 year objectives · Annual improvement priorities · Targets to improve · Resource deliveries down below 10%. The second year's target was to bring it below 5%. The organization is now exceeding its expectations on product delivery, so the leadership team is reevaluating whether this high level indicator should remain as a corporate priority. Perhaps it is time that this indicator be delegated to daily management to maintain the gains.

Customer feedback now tells them that delivery of prototypes is an emerging issue with the move toward more custom processes. This new indicator may replace the old indicator in future planning cycles, if it rises to the top of the filtering process in the next planning cycle as a vital success factor to achieving customer satisfaction.

This example shows the dynamic nature of the hoshin planning process. As the environment changes and the organization's capabilities increase, so do the hoshins change. Once the company elevates its capability in a hoshin area, it is no longer a breakthrough strategy. Rather, the capability becomes "business as usual." This illustrates the relationship between annual hoshin objectives and daily management. Through the hoshin planning system, the leadership aligns the organization's goals and objectives with changes in the environment and its key performance gaps.

While most companies select one to three annual hoshins, Texas Instruments selects six to eight annual hoshins and then sets one above all others. Ron McCormick of the Semiconductor Group describes their process:

> We set annual goals for each metric that tracks our five-year stretch goals. Then we take one of the annual objectives and make it the key priority for the year. We tie a portion of the compensation of the top management team to this particular annual goal. For example, we might have eight things we track: on-time delivery, quality, customer satisfaction, new products on time, etc. But one year we tied the executive compensation to on-time delivery, looking for a 50% reduction in line items we failed to ship on time that year. As a result, we dropped late shipments by 75% in one year. In the next year, we tied the compensation to order-fulfillment cycle time and we improved cycle time by 60% in the next two years. This way, one annual objective gets breakthrough improvement. The other annual objectives aim for continuous "stretch" improvement toward the five-year goal.

We will look at the link between the annual objective setting process and employee appraisals in Chapter 5. What is important here is that the senior leadership uses a systematic repeatable process for setting measurable mid-term breakthrough objectives and translating them into a small set of measurable annual priorities.

Some people believe that each annual objective should involve the whole organization. But this ignores an essential principle of hoshin management: "Let the environment drive the organization's activities." To align the organization with changes in the environment, the hoshin management system selects the vital few strategic priorities *before* specifying departmental goals. As a result, some hoshins may require widespread participation. Others will involve only a portion of the organization. Observes Lois Gold of Hewlett-Packard:

> It is very possible that in any given year, a piece of the organization may not contribute to a particular hoshin. This is where many organizations initially go wrong with hoshin planning: they think that everybody needs to be involved every year. To accomplish this, either the hoshins become so vanilla, or organizations try to force fit their planning process to the priorities. At HP, if an organization does not contribute to the overall presidential hoshin, then, in a sense, they have license to hunt after their own issues. Because they still have resources, they still need to do planning. They just don't have to divert some of their resources to the overall hoshin. In a manner of speaking, they can develop their own hoshins.

Warren Evans of Intel observes:

> When we began the hoshin planning process, I initially believed that at least one annual hoshin should be a means that a large part of the organization could contribute to. I call this type of deployment the everybody-in-the-pond deployment. Examples include customer satisfaction, and "six sigma." The objective gives everybody a chance to see how their group might contribute. The target is fuzzy. Everybody can shoot at it, nobody misses, but you don't know if you hit it. Over the last several years, I have grown away from this. My philosophy today is to pick hoshins that are measurable at the top of the organization.

In the end, the purpose of this phase of the planning cycle is to develop concentrated annual policies that drive toward measurable mid-term breakthroughs. The case for keeping it simple and focusing on a chosen few is clear: If you never focus, you will dissipate energy and waste precious resources. Customer focused priorities and effective leadership are critical to orchestrating a strategic breakthrough.

3

Create a Company-Wide Plan of Attack:

Align People, Activities, and Resources Behind those Things that Matter Most to the Organization

Controlling your destiny requires two things: a reasonable understanding of how the competitive world is evolving and a profound understanding of the cause and effect relationships between the things you do and the results that are achieved.
— John Fly of Milliken & Company

The best laid plans leave nothing to chance. Unfortunately, too few organizations take this seriously. When asked "How did you intend to achieve your stated objectives?" many CEOs answer, "By asking everyone to interpret the priorities and do their best." These same leaders wonder why, when they flip the switch at the top of the organization, the lights don't go on below.

Numerous factors can cause a breakdown in circuitry so that the "lights don't go on." The leadership may fail to communicate key elements of the strategy to front line employees: employees may misinterpret the objectives; departments may develop incompatible action plans; division managers may realize, several months into the plan, that they simply don't have the capabilities to meet the objectives.

To avoid these pitfalls, the hoshin planning process requires that organizations develop a detailed, integrated, company-wide plan of attack. Before they ever go to work, managers and subordinates take time to clarify expectations, align contributions, and verify capabilities to ensure that everyone knows what to do and how to work together.

TRADITIONAL CASCADING METHODOLOGIES ARE UNRELIABLE

"Well," you might be thinking, "we routinely establish annual objectives for our employees. These are negotiated between boss and subordinate. What's so different here?"

Many organizations do establish local objectives, but the way in which they set them increases the likelihood of error during implementation. Too often:

• *People plan for other people.* The employees closest to the realities of the business are left out of the planning process or are overridden. This can lead to poor commitment and unrealistic plans.

• *Leaders gamble on the skills of individual employees.* From one boss to the next, personalities and style dictate the techniques and the methods. The result can be arbitrary and unreliable strategies.

• *There is insufficient vertical and horizontal alignment.* Senior management never knows if, when combined, local plans will be sufficient to achieve the top-level requirements.

These and other limitations of traditional cascading methodologies create an unreliable system for executing strategic breakthroughs.

Three Management Principles Help to Align the Organization

Hoshin deployment takes a three-pronged approach to align employees, activities, and resources with those things that matter most to the organization. Specifically, hoshin deployment relies on three management principles:

- *Ask the people who will be responsible for implementing the plan to design the plan.* Senior management uses consensus and team review, not one-way directives, to deploy strategic priorities.
- *Specify the means, not just the results.* Employees and their managers use facts and analysis to select the vital few strategies that they will use to close the critical few performance gaps.
- *Use indicators to ensure vertical and horizontal linkage.* Employees systematically verify that their local plans add up to close the vital few strategic gaps.

Let's take a look at each of these practices in more detail.

ASK EMPLOYEES TO DESIGN THE PLAN

Hoshin deployment operates on the principle that individuals should make their own commitments. The process of making things happen never belongs to top management; it belongs to those who are responsible for executing the plan. So, in hoshin deployment, top management identifies the vital few strategic gaps, but does not tell *how* employees should close them. Teams design their own plans, teams review their own progress, and teams communicate with other teams to ensure alignment and coordination.

Since hoshin deployment views personnel as partners, employee participation becomes an indirect means to clarify understanding, build consensus, and gain commitment to action. Employees know the realistic capability of the system and processes. And, only senior management can ensure resource adequacy. Together, employees and their management can create an ambitious plan based on the realistic capabilities of the organization.

Employee participation produces higher quality decisions. It eliminates the I-could-have-told-you-so's; it puts the responsibility for improvement in the hands of those capable of affecting performance; it leverages intimate knowledge of key business processes; and it builds group commitment to the desired outcomes.

The benefits of employee participation are undeniable. Better decisions, increased commitment, and early detection of potential pitfalls give companies with a participative planning process a competitive advantage over more autocratic ones.

Use the Catchball Process to Reduce Ambiguity

To reduce ambiguity and misinterpretation during the planning process, hoshin management uses a fact-based inter-level negotiation system. Called "catchball," this participative process uses iterative planning sessions to field questions, clarify priorities, build consensus, and ensure that strategies, objectives, and measures are well understood, realistic and sufficient to achieve the objectives. The word "catchball" denotes a Japanese game in which a circle of young children throw a baseball back and forth. It metaphorically describes a planning process where objectives and the means and measures to accomplish them are tossed back and forth between layers in the management hierarchy until consensus is reached. (See Figure 3.1)

In short, catchball is a disciplined multi-level planning methodology for "tossing an idea around." It takes strategic issues to the grassroots level, asking employees at each level of management to "value add" to the plan based on data analysis and experience of their functional areas.

In some companies like Hewlett-Packard, the word *catchball* describes a formal deployment with checkpoints and deadlines through-

Figure 3.1. Use catchball to refine, align, consolidate, and coordinate commitments.

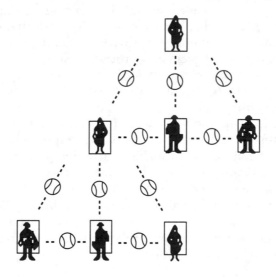

out the planning process. Other companies use the term casually to describe a joint analysis. In all cases, however, catchball requires that the people who deploy downward engage in some kind of data-based conversation with the people who design the plans. There must be sufficient coupling and discussion during the planning process to ensure that the strategic priorities are clear and realistic.

SPECIFY THE MEANS AND MEASURES

Hoshin deployment goes beyond stating desired outcomes to specify the vital few strategies and indicators that will be used to achieve the results. In other words, hoshin deployment requires that employees make visible the cause and effect *behaviors* that will drive their results. When managers take the time to work with their employees to understand and document the process that will be used to execute the plan, they can verify that their organization is truly capable of achieving its stretch objectives.

Specifying the vital few methods by which we hope to achieve our stated objectives is one significant difference between traditional planning methodologies such as MBO and hoshin deployment. Traditional planning systems specify desired outcomes, such as "increase sales by 20%" but abdicate responsibility for the "how." In hoshin planning, employees at every level of the hierarchy specify and document the vital few means or methods that will drive the 20%. Then they establish indicators to track progress toward the objective.

Use a Standardized Process to Select the Supporting Means and Measures

At every level of the hierarchy, employees use facts and root cause analysis to select the vital few means and measures to close strategic gaps. Many managers fret that employee input will be uninformed, antagonistic, obstinate, and/or demanding during the planning process. But when employees are given a reliable set of rules and methods for selecting their strategies, their knowledge improves the quality of the implementation plans. They can justify their plans by demonstrating the logic that will drive their results.

Again, the concepts of "vital" and "few" play a critical role in the planning process. So employees use the same analytic principles and tools to identify their local strategies that the senior management used to set the direction in the early stages of planning.

Key steps in the deployment process include:

- Review the high-level objective, indicator, and goal.
- Form a team.
- Determine the gap between the current situation and the goal.
- Study the sources of error.
- Identify the vital few factors that cause the gap.
- Select the means/strategies for closing the gap.
- Establish appropriate indicators.
- Negotiate the plan details.

These steps move employees from awareness to action.

Some readers will recognize this selection process as an elaboration of the first four steps of the seven-step root cause problem solving process from the school of total quality management (TQM). This process will be discussed more fully in Chapter 4. Suffice it to say that at any point in time employees focus on those means and measures that will eliminate the root cause barriers to progress. (See Figure 3.2.) They identify the vital few strategic gaps that must be closed at their own level to close the higher level strategic gaps. And they develop indicators to track progress.

Regardless of the precise problem-solving methodology, the intention is to provide employees with a set of guidelines to select the vital few necessary and sufficient means to be recorded in the company-wide annual plan. Such a disciplined approach builds an organizational capability, a consistent and repeatable process, not simply a reliance on personnel, to execute strategic priorities.

Standardize the Planning Vocabulary

Another hoshin deployment tool is the use of standardized vocabulary to link words with numbers. Shared vocabulary increases the quality and speed with which employees can communicate and negotiate local plans.

Some companies (Procter & Gamble, for example) use the terms "objectives," "goals," "strategies," and "measures" (OGSM) to describe the relationship between corporate priorities and the methods used to achieve them. Other organizations (Zytec, for example) use the

Figure 3.2. Use root cause analysis to close gaps.

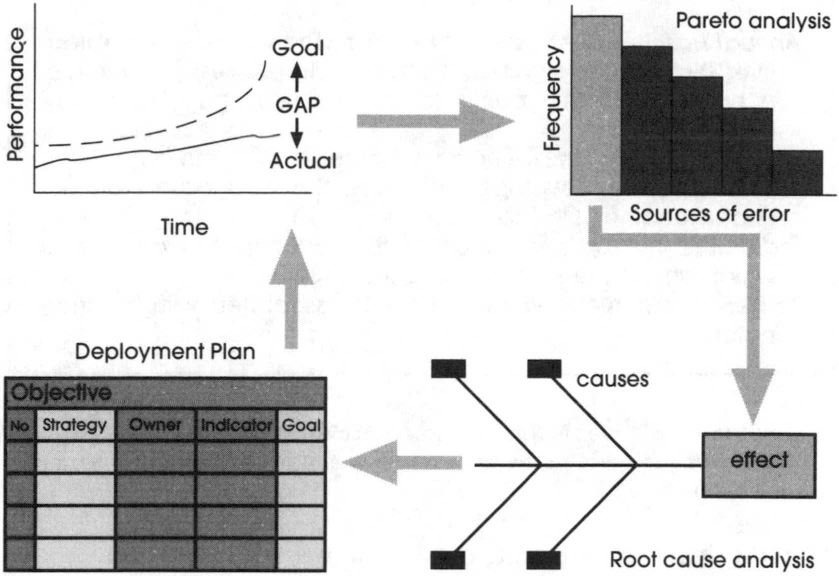

words "targets" and "means." This briefing uses the vocabulary shown in the box, page 84. Regardless of the vocabulary, the basic management concept is the same: *Control the outcome and also the methods used to achieve the desired outcome.*

Moreover, most companies ask their employees to state their hoshin strategies in a formal manner. Typically, the format goes as follows:

- the objective (cascaded from above)
- the means
- the direction of improvement (reduce, establish, improve, eliminate, etc.)
- the numerical indicators to track progress
- the target or goal for each indicator
- the completion date

For example, the strategy to "meet or exceed a rating of 9.5/10 on the customer satisfaction index by Q4" (objective) might read like this:

OBJECTIVES vs. STRATEGIES

Annual Hoshin Objectives, or "*Hoshins*": The two or three objectives that require significant changes in process or structure. A hoshin objective points to the specific "gap" that must be closed.

Hoshin Strategies: The behaviors that lead us to the objectives. Strategies are developed to close the gap based on our understanding of the situation.

Indicators: The units of measure that quantify the degree to which we are meeting our stated objectives.

Targets: The numeric values or goals associated with the indicators.

Implement just-in-time (means) to reduce (direction) cycle time as measured in days (indicator) by two (target) by end of fourth quarter (completion date).

In short, it is not sufficient to state the means to close the gap in words. Employees establish at least one indicator, or measure, for each means. Together, the means and measures determine whether the local plan is sufficient to achieve the higher level objectives.

Use a Standardized Planning Matrix to Document and Communicate the Commitments

Plans cannot be managed or negotiated unless they are documented. If there is no record of commitments, memory lapses create unnecessary variability and impede planning and implementation.

To prevent such lapses, hoshin management uses a standardized annual deployment matrix to document and communicate strategies. This matrix records key assumptions and commitments made in creating the action plan. It also forms the basis for review at later points throughout the year.

While there are a variety of formats, annual planning tables generally include certain pieces of information:

- The identity of the business unit
- The author and owner of the plan
- A column to list each annual objective and its goal

- Number references for the objectives
- A column to reference the number of each strategy to achieve the objective
- A column to record the strategies and the owner of these sub-strategies
- A column to list the metrics or indicators for each strategy

Figure 3.3 shows an annual planning table from Hewlett-Packard. Note the simplicity of format for capturing and recording this important information. Such a form provides a paper trail to link the local objectives with the assumptions and long-term strategic issues. This information not only helps to deploy the breakthrough objectives to others in the organization but also records the key assumptions to be reviewed in the next annual planning cycle.

CREATE VERTICAL AND HORIZONTAL LINKAGE, NOT JUST A COUPLING BETWEEN LAYERS

A company-wide effort to close strategic gaps will generate a myriad of local plans. Yet, in too many companies, local plans are created,

Figure 3.3. Use a planning table to document key elements.

Prepared by: Soo Kok Leng	Date:	Fiscal year:	Division:	Location/ Department: Manufacturing	
Situation: Market forces and the industry learning curve require declining prices for our parts, if we are to remain cost competitive. Increased sales volumes are needed to reach profit goals. These two factors require substantial reduction in manufacturing cost.					
Objective	NO.	Strategy (Owner)		Performance measure	
3.1.6 Define plans for 20% reduction in part cost from (date) to (date) Target/goal 1. 3.0 months of inventory (balanced with corporate guidelines) 2. 20% reduction in part cost from (date)	.1 .2 .3	Control non-labor expenses (all managers) Reduce world wide cycle time to cut inventory costs (scheduling. wfr fab. die fab. ICS managers) Improve organization and processes/procedures for higher productivity (all managers)		Actual expenses = 90% FY90 target – cycle time – months of inventory – 30% DL and 10% IDL cost reduction – 2% cost reduction by process simplification	

but they are not integrated. Employees may design fully appropriate plans at the local level only to find that these plans are incompatible with plans that other groups design. Problems arise when people, activities, and resources begin to interact during the implementation phase.

A key principle of hoshin deployment is vertical and horizontal linkage. Specifically, a disciplined alignment methodology ensures that:

1. local objectives are vertically and horizontally aligned, and
2. the organization is capable of delivering the desired results.

To establish this linkage, managers develop, share, and negotiate their plans to support their superior's stated contribution in conjunction with those of interrelated functions.

While each company customizes its linkage system, three planning steps characterize a typical hoshin deployment process. These include:

- *Cascade the annual hoshin objectives.* Senior managers vertically communicate the vital few annual business objectives and their indicators to all employees who can make a quantitative contribution.
- *Negotiate the means and measures.* Employees use facts and analysis to develop and coordinate their strategies and indicators with peers and managers.
- *Roll-up the plans.* Managers at each level of the hierarchy consolidate local plans to verify that they are sufficient to achieve their superior's stated contribution.

The cascading process ensures clarity at the local level. The negotiation process develops realistic local plans to which employees feel committed. The roll-up process verifies that the collective set of local plans will indeed deliver the corporate requirements. Together, the cascading, negotiation, and roll-up processes align the organization behind those things that matter most to the organization: You get vertical alignment on the way down and horizontal alignment on the way up. Only after the high-level objectives are cascaded and the detailed plans are rolled-up is the corporate plan considered to be final.

CASCADE STRATEGIC REQUIREMENTS

A disciplined cascading process provides a mechanism whereby employees can receive vital strategic information from above to feed development of their local strategies, thereby creating vertical integration. It incorporates the annual corporate objectives into each department manager's annual plan. Thus, implementing the departmental plan helps to achieve the company objectives. The degree to which this process is standardized and continually improved increases the quality of the local strategies.

Start with the Big Picture

A successful deployment begins with a description of the big picture. If employees are familiar with the vision and strategic issues, they are more likely to develop consistent and appropriate plans. In hoshin deployment, leaders go first to their direct reports to communicate the story behind the strategic objectives. They build the case for the vision and review the overall purpose of the long-term strategy. They talk about the rationale behind the breakthrough objectives. They describe senior management's criteria for success, including a time frame and the challenges to pulling it off. They describe the annual hoshin objectives, the indicators, and the targets. In other words, they "tell a story" about why, what, how, and how much.

A compelling story helps leaders to communicate strategies in three ways. First, it enables stakeholders to discover a personal relationship to the corporate objective. This builds commitment and motivation. Second, the story expands the horizon of awareness. Employees can better understand how solving a local problem may help to achieve a hoshin objective. Third, it provides a mental model in which to make sense of new information, retain it longer, and integrate day-to-day activities with a collective purpose.

Choose a Cascading Protocol

Once employees understand and accept the big picture, they can identify their role in achieving the strategic objectives. Using root cause analysis, employees translate the high level strategic gaps into the vital few measurable contributions at their own level. But, who goes first? How do teams form around the high-level objectives? What is the choreography behind the planning process?

Cascading protocols differ by company. Some companies cascade their annual policies on a functional basis. The leadership of one organization may ask broadly that everyone determine how their group might contribute to the achievement of a breakthrough objective. For instance, the leadership at Florida Power & Light deploys their objectives to the entire organization, then it asks what each group can contribute to the strategy. Employees formally submit their ideas and the leadership determines which of these ideas the organization will pursue. In contrast, Procter & Gamble deploys its annual objectives by targeting particular groups based on their knowledge of what needs to be done.

Other organizations deploy their annual objectives in a cross-functional fashion. For instance, if the annual objective is to increase market share, one strategy might be to improve the performance of the product. This strategy could be deployed vertically to the research and development team. Another opportunity might be to cut the time to market in half for new products. This might call for the product development, purchasing, manufacturing, and engineering departments to work together in order to eliminate those problems that occur during hand-offs between functions. It is not uncommon for the outcome of an annual hoshin to be a redesign.

Whether the organization chooses to cascade functionally or cross-functionally, the objective is the same: Communicate the measurable strategic requirements, but not how the gaps must be closed. Let teams of employees at the next level down review the situation and determine at their own level how the gaps can be closed.

Vertically Link the Local Plans

To ensure vertical integration, many companies link their activities downward in an ends-means-ends-means fashion. In other words, the desired outcome of each level in the hierarchy becomes the target for the means at the next lower level of the hierarchy. At each level of the organization, objectives (ends) are received from above, and strategies (means) are designed from below and sideways to achieve these objectives.

Often, companies use a vertical numbering system to make visible the vertical linkage between objectives and supporting strategies. For example, Objective 1.0 is supported by Strategies 1.1, 1.2, 1.3, etc. Strategy 1.1 is supported by Sub-strategies 1.11, 1.12, 1.13 and so on.

This type of deployment is different from a deployment of just numbers, which is characteristic of traditional planning methodologies such as MBO. (See Figure 3.4.) Traditional planning methodologies cascade results, often in the same units of measure. In contrast, hoshin deployment customizes the metrics to fit the means. As the objectives cascade down the organization, the units of measure change accordingly. (See Figures 3.5 and 3.6.)

Both Hewlett-Packard and Florida Power & Light are well known for this method of deployment. Once top management defines the key objectives, it then cascades those objectives to the next layer of management. The individuals who are closest to the business define the most appropriate strategies to support these objectives. In other words, this next layer specifies the "how." In selecting supporting strategies, direct reports are careful to take into account their employees' input as well as that of their peers. The goal? To coordinate commitments so as to zero in on the final destination from every conceivable angle.

NEGOTIATE THE MEANS AND MEASURES

A cascading protocol typically improves vertical communication. Alone, however, it ensures neither vertical integration nor horizontal

Figure 3.4. Traditional cascading methodologies emphasize results.

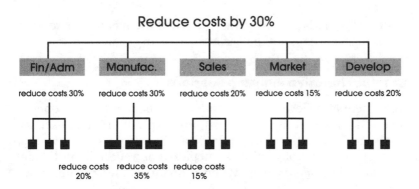

coordination. In the absence of inter-level and cross-functional coordination, local plans may conflict with one another. To improve the quality of their plans, employees needs to negotiate their plan details with other individuals and groups.

Look Upwards and Sideways Before Developing the Plan

Many companies formalize the negotiation process. At Intel, employees focus on the objective cascaded to them from above, then review the boundaries of their business area. Next, they identify their partners (customers, clients, managers, etc.), the products and services for which they are responsible, and their partners' criteria for success (quality, time, cost, effectiveness, etc.). At each level, employees use root cause analysis to identify what prevents them from achieving the high level targets. Indicators naturally emerge as the tools to measure success. Employees document the name, unit of measure, and operational definition of the indicators. Then they develop process-related tactics to close these gaps. (See Figure 3.7 for Intel's worksheet.)

In hoshin deployment, it is important to distinguish measures from goals—a common source of confusion. David Lord of Procter & Gamble observes:

> Dates start showing up as the measures. If I want to put in a new computer system to reduce inventory, a lot of groups might think in terms of the time table to install the system. That's important. But what they really need to measure is whether that computer system achieved the inventory reduction that they had planned.

The value of an indicator is to track how well the means are working to close a strategic gap, not the occurrence of an event.

Conduct Iterative Planning Sessions

Some people believe that agreement can be achieved in one or two planning sessions. But team planning typically requires several iterations in the creative group brainstorming process. On the first pass, employees typically select strategies that reflect a traditional view of their business system. When individuals and organizations

Figure 3.5. Cascade the objectives, means, and measures.

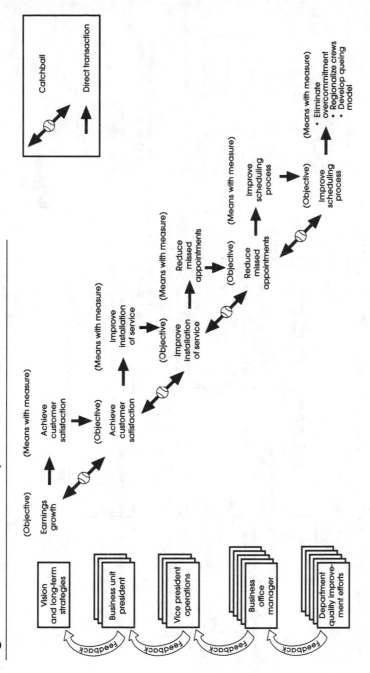

Source: Ward Consulting Group, Inc. Used by permission.

Figure 3.6. Use root cause analysis to develop indicators and link plans.

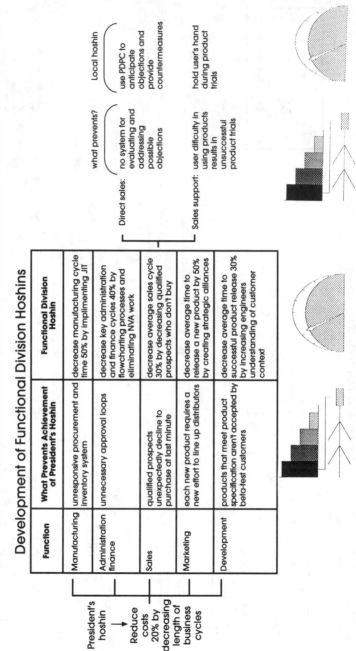

Development of Functional Division Hoshins

Function	What Prevents Achievement of President's Hoshin	Functional Division Hoshin
Manufacturing	unresponsive procurement and inventory system	decrease manufacturing cycle time 50% by implimenting JIT
Administration finance	unnecessary approval loops	decrease key administration and finance cycles 40% by flowcharting processes and eliminating NVA work
Sales	qualified prospects unexpectedly decline to purchase at last minute	decrease average sales cycle 30% by decreasing qualified prospects who don't buy
Marketing	each new product requires a new effort to line up distributors	decrease average time to release a new product by 50% by creating strategic alliances
Development	products that meet product specification aren't accepted by beta-test customers	decrease average time to successful product release 30% by increasing engineers understanding of customer context

President's hoshin

Reduce costs 20% by decreasing length of business cycles

Direct sales:

what prevents? — no system for evaluating and addressing possible objections

Local hoshin — use PDPC to anticipate objections and provide countermeasures

Sales support: user difficulty in using products results in unsuccessful product trials

hold user's hand during product trials

Adapted from *A New American TQM: Four Practical Revolutions in Management*, by Shoji Shiba, Alan Graham, and David Walden. Copyright © 1993 by Center for Quality Management. Published by Productivity Press, Inc., PO Box 13390, Portland, OR 97213-0390, (800) 394-6868. Reprinted by permission.

Figure 3.7. Work with partners to develop indicators and goals.

| MBP Plan Item: | Strategy 3.2 - Meet or exceed a rating of 9.5/10 on the customer satisfaction index by (date). |
| Scope: | - All customers in all market segments
- From initial contact to successful delivery of all products and services |

Partners	Outputs	Partner Success Criteria	Indicators	Goal
Customer interface • Geographies marketing • Sales • CQEs End customers Factories	Components, modules & systems Information	Defect-free products (# of products rejected each month)	# of defect-free products received by customer (%) ──────── # of products shipped ↑	99.5% by (date)
		Products and services delivered on time per our request date yes/no	# of orders received per request date (%) ──────── # of products shipped ↑	98.5% by (date)
			Cycle time (days): Receipt of order to customer acceptance of order ↓	2 days by (date)
	Customer service	Response to requests for information, repairs, analysis, etc. received by our request date yes/no	Cycle time (hours): Request submitted by customer to request closed by customer ↓	24 hours by (date)

S.O. #3 owner		Increase customer satisfaction index rating without exceeding budget	$ expended (%)
			────────
			$ budgeted →
				100% by (date)

repeat the brainstorming process, however, they are apt to more fully challenge prior mental models and paradigms. This is precisely when breakthrough thinking is most likely to occur.

The catchball process encourages employees and their managers to continue the necessary dialogue until they reach consensus. Through iterative planning sessions, erroneous assumptions can be confronted and replaced with more effective ones. Inconsistencies can be reconciled. And scattered information can be brought together into meaningful patterns—all in the spirit of continuous improvement. Lois Gold of Hewlett-Packard observes:

> Even with the managers sitting in a room, it can sometimes take weeks to sort out an operational definition, and that is where catchball comes in—constantly going back for explanation and clarification to make sure that everyone in the organization really understands things. All those who have a part in the planning process participate in a back-and-forth discussion until they agree on the essence of the plan, the targets, and

how the plan will play out in the organization. When these executives go back with their own direct reports, they talk about how they are going to deploy this objective/strategy and what additional ones should be added to contribute to this. This goes for both the manager and his or her subordinates. The question is, "Are the managers articulating the plan in a way that is clear?" Sometimes it seems perfectly clear at the time you are doing it. Yet, someone may ask, "Why are you looking for a 20% reduction in cost." "Is that realistic given where we are sitting this year"? Or, "Do you mean 20% across the board"?

The whole purpose of catchball is constant clarification—to arrive at consensus before you actually go out to implement the plan—so that you really do have alignment. With catchball, you don't have a mere mechanistic deployment. You aim to have everyone in the organization understand what the priorities are, why they exist, and how they are going to contribute before proceeding with the plan. In a matrix organization, catchball becomes even more important to ensure that all the superiors who are influencing a particular manager or function are sending the same priorities down from the top.

Control the Number of Priorities by Level

Cascading targets and means is an effective way to deploy high-level priorities. But, sometimes the descending targets and means can multiply out of control. This is likely to occur in an organization with a matrix structure. Lois Gold of Hewlett-Packard explains:

> HP is a matrix organization. When we first started deployment, we ran into a number of problems. One was that we had individuals getting direction from multiple masters. As the hoshins rolled down the organization, people were ending up with five to ten supporting hoshin objectives, which by definition violates the sense of priority. So, over time, we tried to think of how we could harness the power of hoshin and not necessarily worry about the most pure deployment of it. The goal of hoshin is to articulate, at the highest level, the critical few (one to three) priorities in any given planning year, and then align the organization behind them; that is the key. The implementation plans are a way of mechanically observing the alignment. In a matrix organization, it is particularly important to develop tools which allow you to understand the flow.

In a matrix management structure, an employee may receive seemingly unrelated objectives descending from multiple sources in the hierarchy. For instance, an employee might get the message from one superior that he or she needs to increase market share. Another boss might ask the employee to increase growth.

To limit the number of priorities to a manageable set, Hewlett-Packard developed an additional deployment protocol, called the umbrella method. The umbrella method helps the employee to satisfy two or more objectives by asking the question "What do these objectives have in common"? The subordinate defines a single objective that contributes to both of the descending objectives at a higher level of abstraction. In other words, the descending objectives are treated as causes (think fishbone analysis) of some larger problem.

What are some other things that you can do to prevent the descending objectives from growing too quickly? Hewlett-Packard specifies that no manager be responsible for more than three objectives, and no employee working on a particular objective commits to more than five strategies. If a person ends up with more than five strategies, the manager examines the subordinate's commitments more closely. If the organization is a portfolio organization, then each strategy directs a different piece of the organization. In such situations, not all resources work on all five strategies. Rather, they are working on individual strategies. And the rule of five maximum strategies is reevaluated for its appropriateness.

ROLL-UP THE COMMITMENTS TO VERIFY CAPABILITY

Traditional planning processes stop when objectives are cascaded to the lowest level of the organization. The idea is that "Now that you know what we want, go do it."

In hoshin deployment, the planning is only half over when objectives and means are cascaded from top to bottom. When high-level objectives have been translated into local means and measures, a second process begins, known in some organizations as "roll-up." This process ensures that local plans are coordinated horizontally as well as vertically. It also verifies that taken together, the detailed plans add up to deliver the corporate requirements. It provides bottom-up feedback to the leadership that communicates the message, "Given our resource constraints and experience, this is what we are capable of."

While the cascading process is often a somewhat informal process, communicating the detailed plans upward is more rigorous. In the hoshin roll-up, each higher level manager is responsible for reconciling the plans between the groups below him or her in the hierarchy and across organizational boundaries. The intent is to ensure the most effective utilization of resources. The manager is also responsible for verifying that the contributions from the next lower level will satisfy the requirements specified in his or her contract with the next higher level in the organization. (See Figure 3.8.)

The roll-up is essentially a capability check. The prevailing question is: When we add up all the detailed contributions specified in the implementation plan, does the collective effort meet the annual requirements? The back and forth dialogue of the roll-up process minimizes the gap between business requirements and organizational capability.

Share Individual Matrices

The first step in the roll-up process is for individuals to collectively share their planning matrices with their direct supervision. Together, subordinates and management look for opportunities to:

Figure 3.8. Verify capability of local plans to meet objectives.

Superior's Hoshins

		A	B	C
Subordinate 1	a		☉	
	b		☉	
	c			☉
Subordinate 2	d	☉		
	e			☉
	f		☉	
Subordinate 3	g	☉		
	h			☉
	i			☉

☉ Denotes high impact.

From *A New American TQM: Four Practical Revolutions in Management*, by Shoji Shiba, Alan Graham, and David Walden. Copyright © 1993 by Center for Quality Management. Published by Productivity Press, Inc., PO Box 13390, Portland, OR 97231-0390, (800) 394-6868. Reprinted by permission.

- eliminate redundancies and duplication,
- settle conflicts or contradictions, and
- acknowledge and accumulate resource requirements and constraints.

Important issues might include redundant training activities or travel, timing, or sequence issues, and previously unknown resources and opportunities for improvement. These potential implementation pitfalls are resolved through dialogue and consensus.

Consolidate, Adjust, and Finalize the Plan

The objective of the roll-up phase is to adjust the company plans to reflect this added knowledge. Sequentially, each manager from the bottom of the organization upward creates a single consolidated matrix covering the groups for which he or she is responsible. This matrix is a modified plan based on employee input.

When done properly, this bottom-up consolidation modifies the initial top-down policies. If the local action plans are sufficient to achieve their overall objective and the resource capability is realistic, then the organization can proceed with implementation. But, if the plans are not sufficient (e.g., the contributions do not add up to the total effort required or requirements exceed available resources) then the managers and direct reports who designed the plans must determine what is needed to make them sufficient.

Create a Safe Environment

In the end, hoshin planning is a neutral process; it is only as good as the data you use. If people are afraid to provide accurate information on the real capabilities of the organization, then hoshin planning will yield inappropriate and ineffective strategies.

Many people have a jaundiced view of the objective setting process, a view associated with the MBO process. They are used to recrimination. So, they may initially under-report the capability of the organization or under-commit on targets, for fear of reprisal. They may be reluctant to modify plans during the deployment phase. Consequently, the leadership must work hard to emphasize performance of the system, not simply performance of the individual. Safe and open conditions help employees to reveal relevant yet previously inaccessible information and clarify obscure messages.

As members of the organization gain confidence in the roll-up process, there is typically increased employee contribution. Mr. Sasaoka, President of Yokogawa Hewlett-Packard recalls that during their first year of implementing policy deployment, virtually all directives emanating from top management came back unchanged. Today, he estimates that what is eventually implemented is only sixty percent intact; the remainder is modified according to lower level management input.

TAKE THE TIME TO PLAN

At this point, you may be thinking, "This deployment methodology is nice in theory, but we cannot afford to specify all the details of our implementation process. It will take too much time and is too cumbersome."

These are valid concerns. It does take time. And, at times, it may feel tedious as teams struggle to reach consensus on the detailed means and measures required to support key strategies. But what happens if you do not involve employees in the development of plans that depend on them? What happens if you fail to clarify ambiguous objectives, set realistic targets, and link performance indicators with the strategy?

In the end, a successful organization does what the unsuccessful organization is unwilling to do. In the case of hoshin deployment, this means participative planning and vertical and horizontal linkage. When we take the time to coordinate local action plans and verify cause and effect, we drive variability out of the implementation process. We don't get just results, we get *planned* results.

Hoshin deployment provides a visible, measurable, practical plan of attack. It translates annual corporate objectives into coordinated quantitative contributions at the local level.

But how do employees control the plan throughout the year? How do they schedule the milestones and activities along the way? This leads us to the next chapter, where we look at how to control the plan and ensure a faithful execution.

4

Control the Plan:
Align Daily Activity with the Plan

Navigation is the science of determining the position of a ship, aircraft, or guided missile and charting a course for guiding the craft safely and expeditiously from one point to another.
                                                                —Alfred E. Fiore

A deployment plan translates annual breakthrough objectives into an integrated set of means and measures. But a high-level, company-wide plan alone does not ensue a faithful execution. A lack of detailed action plans, problem-solving capabilities, and/or project management skills can cause well-meaning employees to pursue other activities throughout the year at the expense of the annual plan.

Hoshin management relies on three principles to bring the capability of the business system up to the level required in the deployment plan. Specifically, employees:

- Use the PDSA/SDCA cycles to iteratively zero in on the destination.
- Use root cause analysis to identify and eliminate obstacles to progress.

- Use process control to create a reliable business system that meets strategic requirements.

Let's take a detailed look at each of these management practices.

ITERATIVELY ZERO IN ON THE DESTINATION

In a changing environment, it is difficult if not impossible to execute any plan as originally conceived. Initial assumptions about resources, time, and personnel may prove inadequate; unexpected problems arise, and so on. Employees need a flexible yet disciplined management process, one that is capable of creating mid-course corrections.

A mini-version of the PDSA (Plan-Do-Study-Act) cycle is used together with SDCA (Standardize-Do-Check-Act) cycle to make gains in process performance during the execution phase and prevent backward slippage. In other words, employees use the same PDSA concept to manage the commitments they made during the deployment phase. Once an improvement is made, the group standardizes that level of performance as a platform for the next round of improvements.

Repeated rotation of these cycles throughout the year brings results closer and closer to the desired annual target. As employees and managers solve problems and learn more about the capability of their systems, they fold this new information back into the planning and implementation process.

Setting the Mini-PDSA/SDCA in Motion

The first step in controlling the execution is to create a detailed action plan. By negotiating and specifying details such as who, what, when, and where, employees create a plan—and the plan itself becomes an execution tool.

Some companies, like Milliken, use few forms in their planning process. John Fly, vice president of strategic planning, expresses the rationale for the "virtually paperless" system by asserting, "We want to look into your eyes and know that you have a plan and that you are deeply committed to it."

Most hoshin management companies, however, ask employees to put the details into a written action plan. This plan documents the

PDSA steps that will be taken to implement the strategies or means to support the higher level hoshin objectives. (See Figure 4.1.) As Gold of Hewlett-Packard explains it:

> All the annual hoshin plan does is communicate the priorities and the logic. The guts of the larger plan are the implementation plans, in other words, the tactical piece of how we are going to accomplish these things. Here at HP, the higher level plans come in the form of draft plans so that people can begin to create action plans. Later, there is a formal process of communicating the final plans upward to ensure organizational capability.

When it comes to the execution phase of hoshin management, the question is never "if," but always "how." A detailed plan can clarify important questions: Which steps and actions are needed first? What activities can we do simultaneously? What are our contingency plans? Specifically, the action plans:

Figure 4.1. Many companies use a standardized format to document action plans.

Prepared by A. Furd	Date	Division	Fiscal year :	Location Department		Quality Systems/ Quality Department	
Ref #	**Strategy**	**Implementation Item**	**Respons Person**	**Q1** Nov Dec Jan	**Q2** Feb Mar Apr	**Q3** May Jun Jul	**Q4** Aug Sep Oct
3.1.1	Increase number of departments using TQC process improvement	1. Survey # of processes with PPM metrics	Linda J.	:--- *			
		2. Identify processes with severe performance problems	Linda J.	*			
		3. Meet with mfg mgr to plan TQC process improvement training and follow-up support	Linda J/		p--p		
		4. Assign trainers and coaches to conduct the training	A. Furd/ Linda J.		p--p		
		5. Review trainer's/ supervisor's plans for individual performance goals after training	Linda J.		:-----p		
		6. Develop schedule for conducting the training and providing coaching support	Linda J.			p	

Key: * = Completed   P = Planned   :---> = Activity leading to completion   p---p = Stoppage in Plan

- establish deadlines for each implementation theme,
- sequence critical tasks,
- specify resource requirements,
- establish milestones,
- establish reporting formats, and
- schedule progress reviews.

The more detailed the project plan, the easier it is to manage the project. This is just good project management. John Rogers of Zytec adds:

> Because we have found that strong action plans are crucial to success, we have begun concentrating on review of action plans. We do this by featuring the action plan for one MBP [Management by Planning] objective each month. The manager reviews the status of action plans for each of four MBP objectives three times a year.

Although a variety of formats can be used to standardize the action plan, certain universal pieces of information are typically documented. These include:

- a reference number for the appropriate strategy,
- activities, tasks, actions, and means to achieve the strategy,
- the indicators and goals,
- owners of each activity, and
- a timeline or deadline for each activity.

Taking the time to think through and negotiate these details significantly enhances the probability that members of the organization will achieve what it is that they set out to do.

Use Planning Tools to Create the Detailed Action Plan

Certain planning tools (see Appendix B) help employees move down the ladder of abstraction from the generalities of the hoshin deployment plan to the specific details of the action plan.

The PDPC, or "process decision program chart," for example, is a contingency planning tool, especially useful when a team is doing something for the first time. It is used to troubleshoot plans and identify appropriate countermeasures when the goal, problem, or process is an unfamiliar one. Given the occurrence of an undesirable development, the team will have a "structure" in place for dealing with that development. The PDPC tool helps a team "play the odds" so that it can allocate resources quickly and effectively.

The arrow diagram, sometimes called an activity network diagram, is used to visualize and plan any steps that can be done in parallel. It can be used to schedule and control simultaneous tasks when the subtasks, their sequencing, and duration are well known. The tool helps to identify the appropriate sequence of tasks, which ones can be done in parallel, which tasks are the most critical to monitor, and the total completion time.

Some groups prefer the activity network diagram over a standard Gantt chart. Although the horizontal bars of a Gantt chart depict which tasks can be done simultaneously throughout the project, this tool does not show which tasks are interrelated.

These and other planning tools enable employees to think through the details as part of the execution phase.

Use the Detailed Action Plan to Manage the Execution Phase

The more detailed the action plan, the more reliable the execution will be. The challenge, however, is not to over-engineer the process. Lord of Procter & Gamble provides insight on this point:

> What I find is that there are two kinds of people. One type doesn't like to do a bunch of analysis, so they throw something together and get going. They work on the first thing that comes to mind and soon find out they are not working on the right thing—because they didn't do the analysis. Then you have another group of folks who try to develop the perfect plan, so that they can avoid "doing." A whole year goes by, and there is no action. The answer is to do enough analysis to focus the plan on causes versus outputs, yet not try to have a perfect plan. We want them to start with what is known, then get on with the plan.

The execution phase includes more than just a detailed action plan. The PDSA cycle requires that employees "Do" the plan, then "Study" their progress, and take corrective "Action" as necessary.

Many managers use their action/implementation plan to manage their time. They emphasize the "Check-Act" pieces of the mini-PDCA cycle. Observes Gold of Hewlett-Packard:

At my monthly meetings with my direct reports, their implementation plans are a key part of our discussion because that is our commitment to each other. A lot of managers use their implementation plans, whether it is face-to-face contact or over the phone, as a way of structuring their discussion in terms of the tactical, the real nitty-gritty things. I don't wait for the hoshin review to have discussion for the first time about problems.

The implementation plan becomes an *active management tool*. It translates the annual deployment plan into a series of calendar activities. In other words, it integrates the annual hoshin plan into daily activity, by making the manager's calendar work toward strategic breakthroughs.

SEARCH FOR AND ELIMINATE THE ROOT CAUSE OF EMERGING PROBLEMS

Problems are expected in the course of an implementation. A successful implementation is not determined by the absence of problems. Rather, success is measured by *how* we solve the problems that do emerge.

For this reason, hoshin management uses a standardized problem-solving methodology from the school of total quality management (TQM). It is often called the seven-step "root cause" problem-solving process.

The seven-step problem solving process is a logical, commonsense method to solve any type of problem. It provides a road map to help senior management and other employees solve problems during the improvement journey. It suggests what materials and information are needed to resolve an emergent issue. And it provides a record of the decision-making process. If the solution we select does not bring the desired results, we can review our steps and assumptions and make subsequent adjustments.

Versions of this problem-solving process exist under a variety of acronyms. Regardless of the specific model employed, there are seven universal steps:

1. Select the issue.
2. Search for data to describe the situation.
3. Analyze the facts to obtain the root cause(s) of the performance gap.

4. Select a solution.
5. Conduct a pilot test.
6. Evaluate performance.
7. Standardize the gains, reflect, and repeat the process.

Let's take a look at each of these steps in more detail.

1. Select the Issue. Start with the voice of the customer. If the objective is cascaded from above, consider the objective in the context of what you know about your customers. Even if your workgroup does not have direct contact with the external customer, take the time to identify how your daily activities affect the customer. Then create a measurable problem statement, such as "reduce late deliveries." Specify the measurable performance gap that you wish to close.

2. Search for data to describe the current situation. Gather all the relevant facts. In the early stages of any problem-solving process, data are often scarce, and it's tempting to accelerate the process by moving right to action. But take the time to search for data to describe the current situation. Use the seven quality tools (fishbone diagram, Pareto chart, histogram, line chart, scatter diagram, control chart, and check sheets) to analyze the data and visually display the facts of the story. New ways of thinking will emerge when the data have a chance to speak.

3. Analyze the facts to obtain the root cause(s). Problems are often complex. Often, what we view as a problem is merely the symptom of a deeper, more complex problem with multiple contributing factors. In other words, the problem manifests in one area, but the "root cause(s)" of the problem lies elsewhere. One simple method to identify the root cause of a problem is called the "five whys." Simply ask "why?" five times. By the time you get to the fifth "why," you are usually down to bedrock. Another technique used to identify root causes is the fishbone diagram (also called the Ishikawa diagram, or the cause and effect diagram). The main purpose of the technique is to identify and map the major contributing factors to the development of a problem.

4. Select a solution. Unlike many mathematical problems, which allow for only one answer, quality problems have many possible solutions. So don't jump to the conclusion that one particular solution is the only solution. Take the time to identify and consider as many ideas as possible. This is perhaps the most creative step in the problem solving process. Do not judge the quality of your solutions, even the crazy ones, until you exhaust the brainstorming process. Then, select an approach, preferably one that focuses on process improvement that is financially feasible, has the best chance of being implemented, and will have a high impact on the problem.

5. Conduct a pilot test. Take the time to do a test run on the solution. Make individual responsibilities clear and establish a daily schedule for the improvement plan. Notify anybody who might be affected by your changes before you begin implementation.

6. Evaluate performance. How well have you done? Is the problem subsiding? Do you see any improvement? Are there any assumptions that need to be modified? Check whether your "solution" produced the desired effect. If the results are not satisfactory, revisit the earlier steps in this problem solving process.

7. Standardize the gains, reflect, and repeat. Once you see that the solution is working, take action to maintain the gain. Standardize the solution so that you can prevent the very improvements you worked so hard to accomplish from being neglected or replaced over time with past practices. Gather data until the benefits stabilize. After you confirm that you achieved your desired effect, communicate the improvement.

The seven-step problem solving process is a powerful mechanism to solve problems once and for all. In the end, an improvement is never an improvement until every step, including follow up, is implemented. Then look for new ways to improve. Continuous improvement is just that—continuous.

IMPROVE AND CONTROL THE PROCESS

Process control is closely related to performance improvement. Many people see solutions as one-time events. Yet most errors are generated by poorly designed processes, and these errors will linger until the process is changed.

A process is any series of steps or activities that adds value by converting inputs into outputs for a customer. Inputs can include such things as supplies, information, and energy. Outputs can be anything from information in reports or data, to services or products. The quality of the process is ultimately judged by the customer's perception of the output.

Many people initially think of a production process in a manufacturing company. But service organizations have processes too. Operational processes include filling a customer order, processing a ticket, making a sales call, or resolving a complaint. Business processes include accounts payable, processing data, and preparing promotional campaigns. Administrative processes include annual planning, budgeting, hiring personnel, and training.

Eliminate Unwanted Variation

Inevitably, the output of every process has variation. The degree of variation depends on the quality of the inputs and the actual design of the process. To minimize unwanted variations, some people try to control the quality of the output though inspection. In a manufacturing setting, this activity may appear in the form of a last-minute inspection before the shipment goes out the door. If the product meets specification, then it is shipped. Otherwise it is discarded or returned for rework. In a financial services setting, this activity may appear in the form of an approval or authorization protocol. If the forms look okay, they are approved. Otherwise they are sent back for rework.

Inspection is not a fundamental solution. While we may catch the errors, the most we can do is fix the problems after the fact. We have not prevented them from occurring in the first place. For this reason, hoshin management goes after the design of the process, not simply the unhappy event. Observes Lois Gold of Hewlett-Packard:

> When organizations first begin to implement hoshin planning, people tend to be project oriented rather than process oriented. You do see an evolution, but it takes three to five years. Doing hoshin planning well requires process sophistication. So some organizations do the two things in parallel; they develop their process management skills at the same time that they are maturing their hoshin management.

To improve the quality of the output of a process, employees need to identify and remove two sources of variation: special cause variation (i.e., that caused by special events outside the process) and common cause variation (caused by the process itself).

Employees again apply the SDCA/PDSA cycles for continuous improvement and the seven-step root cause problem solving process. As Shoji Shiba, Alan Graham, and David Walden point out in *The New American TQM: Four Practical Revolutions in Management* (Productivity Press, 1993), the steps are as follows:

> SDCA—Operate the current process. Identify the common cause variation and the special cause variation.
> PDSA—Find and remove the sources of special cause variation.
> SDCA—Run the new process. Eliminate the sources of any out-of-control variation that begins to occur.
> PDSA—Use the root cause problem solving process to find and eliminate the largest source of common cause variation.
> SDCA—Continue running the new process. Eliminate the source of any out-of-control condition that begins to occur.

Many people initially believe that process control eliminates creativity. This is not the case. Being in control of a process doesn't mean we cannot subsequently improve it. Rather, the challenge is to balance process control with the dedication to continuously improve the standardized process, based on changing internal and external circumstances.

Elevate the Capability of the System

Process improvement provides the link between the annual breakthrough objectives and daily management. Once employees elevate the system capability to the level specified in the hoshin deployment plan, the standardized process becomes part of daily management. Likewise, an existing system capability may be elevated to the status of a breakthrough objective due to its strategic importance.

For example, production lead time may currently be four weeks. To achieve a strategic position in a foreign market, the product lead time must be reduced to two weeks. Once this level of performance is achieved, it becomes part of daily management, i.e., business as usual. This continues until such time that product lead time again is identified as having strategic importance.

This is the purpose of the execution phase—to bring the system or key business processes in line with the new business requirements.

SUMMING IT UP

When we rigorously control the execution phase, we learn what worked and why. We can elevate the capability of our systems and processes to meet the strategic requirements. Yet how does the organization take advantage of the lessons learned? How can employees communicate local lessons upward in the hierarchy to inform future rounds of annual planning? How can they communicate with senior management regarding chronic unresolved problems? This leads us to the next chapter, where we look at how the hoshin management system helps to create a learning organization.

5

Conduct the Hoshin Audit:

Channel Local Lessons Upward to Inform Future Rounds of Planning

The fuel of life is new information—novelty—ordered into new structures. We need to have information coursing through our systems, disturbing the peace, imbuing everything it touches with new life." —Margaret J. Wheatley

It's Monday morning, and Larry is on his way to work at a traditional organization. Today is his annual performance review, and he is nervous. He's worked hard this year. But with the recent changes in his industry and the departure of his old boss, his current activities bear little resemblance to the objectives outlined for him last year. He is particularly uncomfortable because his new boss, Joe, seems irritable lately.

Joe, too, is in the same traffic flow heading into town, and he is also thinking about Larry's performance review. "I wonder if he met any of his objectives?" Joe muses. "I can't remember what they were. I need to review them over coffee before he arrives. Besides, I wonder if Larry is really up to this job. Ever since I arrived in this new position, he seems unfocused and nervous."

Unfortunately for Larry and Joe—and for their organization—this review will involve a great deal of posturing and very little learning. They may exchange some information, but not in any way that supports the strategic planning process.

Larry and Joe are not the only managers who suffer the "annual performance review." Every day, hundreds of managers and their direct reports in corporate America participate in this annual dance. Bosses posture. Employees posture. And the organization still reels out of control.

ANNUAL REVIEWS PROVIDE INSUFFICIENT FEEDBACK

When conducted properly, an individual annual performance review can enhance employee development. But when it comes to capturing and distilling local lessons in ways that inform future rounds of planning, the traditional review provides little useful feedback at the system level. David Lord of Procter & Gamble summarizes the shortcomings:

> At some point there is an output review. If the results are not okay, then the leader says you have to work harder and try harder. Other times, the results may look like they are achieved, but they are not really done. Leaders need to understand what is really going on in the organization. They need to not only understand the result, but also what it is that is getting the result.

A performance review needs to go beyond motivating employees to give more of themselves to the institution. It must interlace work and learning to systematically incorporate each year's lessons into future planning cycles. It must capture and communicate results in ways that help employees and senior managers to take appropriate action as quickly as possible.

CREATE A LEARNING ORGANIZATION

Activities and results work best when they link in a reciprocal relationship. As activities change, so should results. As results change, so should our sequence of activities. The speed with which we receive accurate information about our results improves the quality of our management decisions.

Unfortunately, many organizations have lengthy communications systems. There are significant delays between activities and knowledge of the effects. The longer the delay, the more distorted the view of the market, the work environment, internal and external challenges, and opportunities. Ex-congressman T.V. Smith once described this lag between "knowing" and taking appropriate action by referring to an anonymous poem:

> There was a dachshund once, so long
> He hadn't any notion
> How long it took to notify
> His tail of his emotion;
> And so it happened, while his eyes
> Were filled with woe and sadness,
> His little tail went wagging on
> Because of previous gladness.

Like the dachshund, too many organizations naively pursue outdated and uninformed strategies. As a result, they take corrective action prematurely only to create "overkill" later on. They overcompensate with aggressive behavior aimed at the symptoms of a problem, only to create an even more unstable system.

Certain organizations attempt to minimize the delays between activities and their knowledge of the effect. They work to improve the speed with which they receive information critical to their business. So they create a management system that safely delivers and confronts all parties on discrepancies and gives them sufficient information on what to do about the deficiencies. Confrontation and feedback are the secrets to selecting informed and appropriate strategies.

Some people call this a learning organization. A learning organization is an agile and responsive management system that makes knowledge and knowledges productive. It continuously improves its processes for communicating, monitoring, and correcting deviations from plan so that it can iteratively zero in on its strategic targets and change those targets as needed.

Six practices improve the quality and speed of communication:

1. Treat every employee as a learning agent for the organization.
2. Channel local insights upward.

3. Study failure.
4. Evaluate the methods, not the personnel.
5. Conduct regular and frequent reviews.
6. Use facts and analysis to support conclusions.

Let's take a look at each of these in detail.

Treat Every Employee as a Learning Agent for the Organization

Too often, managers indulge in an underlying arrogance toward their subordinates. This is particularly evident in their attitude toward employees who work at the boundary of the organization.

Boundary agents—service representatives, bank tellers, administrative assistants, attendants, and others—are sources of strategic information. While they may be at the bottom of the hierarchy, these employees typically have the most customer contact, are closest to the realities of the business and to the sources of problems, and are privy to experiences and information of strategic importance.

Consider your own reaction to an intimidating authority figure. Have you ever concealed knowledge of conflicts or problems from your supervisor or others because they are "undiscussable"? Have you ever withheld negative information from someone at work for fear of a direct confrontation or retaliation? Have you ever relied on ambiguous policies to avoid a direct confrontation?

Interactions like these create and reinforce conditions for error. Hidden information remains hidden, ambiguous messages are never clarified, and inconsistent policies go unrevised. When employees are afraid to share information, the organization cannot correctly diagnose and replace ineffective operating practices with more effective ones. In the absence of trust, employees are unable to act in the best interests of the organization.

For this reason, the hoshin review emphasizes shared information. Through open and joint inquiry, employees and managers learn to confront erroneous assumptions and practices and replace them with more effective ones. Inconsistencies are resolved and ambiguous policies are clarified—all in the spirit of continuous improvement.

Channel Local Insights Upward

Diverse perspectives naturally arise through joint inquiry. And it can be a real challenge to learn how to hold and act upon conflicting perspectives simultaneously. Yet we increase our knowledge when we suspend judgment and study the discrepancies.

Too many managers are unwilling to be challenged. They are afraid of the diverse perspectives that arise through joint inquiry.

At one troubled advertising firm, the CEO stood before his division managers and reviewed the company's dismal financial performance. Revenues paled compared with projected bookings, and all the participants were genuinely discouraged. A courageous division manager suggested that the divisions were under pressure to make their projected bookings look as optimistic as possible; perhaps this could account for the inflated estimates. Angered at the suggestions that the sales forecasts were inaccurate, the CEO demanded that any division manager who did not have complete confidence in his or her projections stand before the group—a deliberate and humiliating challenge. Only the division manger who spoke up had the courage to stand.

Few divisions met plan that quarter, and the company went into a management spin. The result: a 25% reduction in force, a corporate review of the forecasting system, an executive memo defining "certain" bookings, and a radical revision of the annual plan to discount the previous inflated bookings.

Disastrous things can happen when top management doesn't want to hear the truth as others might see it. If top management chooses to ignore accurate information on the real capabilities of the organization, then no planning process will yield appropriate strategies.

This highlights a key difference between inquiry and advocacy. Inquiry requires that participants remain neutral during an exchange. Advocacy, on the other hand, occurs when one party pushes a particular opinion. Being able to balance inquiry and advocacy is critical to creating an effective learning environment.

Study Failure

Three practices can turn negative information into valuable information. These are:

1. *Elicit failure information.* Make an effort to obtain failure information from every member of the organization in a non-threatening manner. Pay particular attention to boundary agents. Get beyond the

emotionality of each "negative" outcome, and make the criteria for achieving the next success explicit.

2. *Manage failure in a longer time frame.* When we operate within an urgent time frame, it's easy to interpret "failure" information as useless. Very often, failure has a funny way of contributing to a future success.

3. *Pay attention to all deviations from plan.* Continually check if you are on schedule. If you are not on schedule, then adjust your plan. But if you are achieving your desired results, don't skip the review. Verify that you are achieving the results *because* of your plan. The purpose of a plan is to get *planned results.*

Many managers initially believe that only negative deviations from the plan should be addressed during a review. But, in hoshin management, positive deviations ("We exceeded our expectations") are reviewed as rigorously as are the negative ones. David Lord of Procter & Gamble explains:

> The sign of a good leader is when he or she arrives at a quarterly review to discover that everything appears to be on track [and asks]. . . "Are you getting those results from your plan?" Sometimes employees are meeting their targets, but they are not following their plan.

Whether the deviation from plan is positive or negative, there are lessons to be learned and assumptions to be revised. And all lessons need to be incorporated in future rounds of planning.

Evaluate the Methods, not the Personnel

Too often, feedback is used more as a weapon than a tool. When results are off the mark, many managers blame the individual rather than take the time to understand the methods behind the results.

Blame will never be a part of a solution. Quality improvement experts believe that 85 to 95% of errors are caused by faulty management systems, not by the individual employee. Learning to see structural processes at work, rather than the individuals or "events," is the starting point for corrective action.

For this reason, a hoshin review goes behind the person and the results to study the process, methods, or planning system that was employed to achieve the results. It studies the question, "What can we do differently that might eliminate this problem?" The objective of the review is to analyze the deviation and decide how to take corrective action, not penalize personnel. David Lord explains:

> We want leaders to look at the *process* of getting the results, not just the results. And that is when you have changed from being an MBO-type organization to a more TQM process-thinking organization. Because of the rigor of the review process, the leaders are seeing a lot more information than they did before.

To improve the methods, the manager must act more like a coach than a police officer. In particular, the manager coaches the process that produces the results. The objective is to work with subordinates to create a disciplined process to guarantee the desired results.

Conduct Regular and Frequent Reviews

In too many organizations, managers treat annual plans as static. They put their plans away, dust them off a year later, and then figure out how close they got. In today's competitive environment, organizations can ill afford surprises in the fourth quarter. Rather, they need a dynamic *rolling plan* that keeps the organization agile and responsive.

Regular and frequent reviews up and down the organization provide everyone with an opportunity to share learnings, reflect on earlier attempts to learn, and create new approaches to defining and solving problems. Specifically, periodic reviews provide:

- top management with an efficient method of staying in touch with the realistic capabilities of the organization,
- employees with the means for imparting knowledge into strategy selection, and
- the organization with the ability to quickly respond to changes in direction.

Timely information on deviations from plan leads to timely corrective action.

In the world of periodic reviews, objectives, strategies, measures, goals, activities, and owners become dynamic; they change as new developments occur. If a new competitor or a new technology emerges that has strategic significance, then regular reviews will enable managers and their subordinates to revise the appropriate sections of the plan. Projects or tactics can be canceled, new ones can be integrated, and resources can be redeployed as circumstances dictate.

Periodic reviews enable the organization to zero in on its destination in an iterative fashion. Through self-diagnosis, shared learnings, and the revision of policies, practices, and procedures, the organization can truly become a learning organization. In the end, the purpose of the review is not to learn once, but to learn how to continue to learn.

Use Facts and Analysis to Support Conclusions

The best reviews are data driven. Metrics help us go from the general to the specific. Rather than attack plans in a hit-or-miss style, facts and root cause analysis enable employees to understand deviations from plan and take appropriate corrective action.

The quality of the review process improves when ideas, thoughts, and opinions are grounded in facts and analysis. Appropriate measurements enhance the quality of the review process. Measures allow us to test our working assumptions. They allow us to recognize and reward improvement, and guide future decisions.

USE A HOSHIN REVIEW SYSTEM TO ACHIEVE PLANNED RESULTS

When we view feedback as a process, not an event, we can work to reduce the delays between cause and effect and our knowledge of these effects. This is simple cycle-time management applied to the planning and implementation process.

Working to reduce the cycle time requires that managers improve their processes for communicating, setting realistic targets, selecting appropriate indicators, monitoring progress, and correcting deviations from plan. The outcome is an agile and responsive management system.

The hoshin review is not a review of personnel. Rather, it is a disciplined multi-tiered review process designed to improve the efficiency and effectiveness of the organization in meeting its goals and objectives. It provides an explicit inter-level knowledge exchange process to:

- encourage adherence to the plan,
- report progress toward goals,
- identify obstacles to progress,
- encourage timely corrective action,
- understand and improve the reliability of the planning system,
- share the best-known methods,
- improve the quality of the initial plans, and
- incorporate any changes in the environment that may alter the strategic direction.

More than an annual event, the hoshin review system demands continual review throughout the year at all levels of the organization. The review meeting is attended by all those members of the organization who have a stake in the plan's accomplishment: the individual who is directly impacted by the outcome, the employees who are responsible for achieving the outcome, and any other indirect stakeholders. A linkage system channels local lessons at the project level up to the strategic objective level to inform the CEO and the top management team.

Reviews start at the project level and roll up to the corporate level. (See Figure 5.1.) Whereas expectations are communicated downward during the deployment phase of hoshin management, progress reviews flow from the bottom of the organization upward to the very top of the hierarchy. The same two levels of the hierarchy that negotiate the plans during the deployment phase are also the ones that review the plans. On a level-by-level basis, managers meet with their direct reports and report upward any significant deviations from plan.

While each company customizes its review process to meet the needs of its culture, the bottom-up review usually consists of three pieces:

- monthly reviews,
- consolidated quarterly reports, and
- an annual review.

The monthly review identifies obstacles to progress and evaluates the need for and assists with early corrective action. The quarterly review

Figure 5.1. Hoshin reviews roll upward.

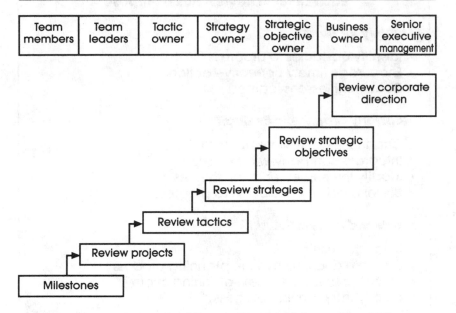

Team members	Team leaders	Tactic owner	Strategy owner	Strategic objective owner	Business owner	Senior executive management

consolidates individual progress reports vertically and horizontally to assess their collective impact on the strategy and group strategic objectives. The annual review evaluates overall progress toward corporate objectives, the reliability of the planning and deployment system, and any new developments in the external environment that might modify the existing goals and objectives. (See box, page 120.)

The whole power of hoshin is that you are not locked into a plan that is not working. If employees discover a failure during the review phase, then they can change the plan and communicate these changes up and down the organization. After all, the review is just one part of the continuous PDSA cycle for continuous improvement.

CONDUCT MONTHLY REVIEWS TO ENCOURAGE TIMELY CORRECTIVE ACTION

Monthly reviews keep employees focused on the hoshin requirements. The monthly review is actually the "Study" phase of the

Each Level of Review Has a Purpose

Monthly Reviews

- Identify obstacles to progress
- Encourage timely corrective action
- Document lessons learned

Quarterly Diagnostic Evaluation

- Channel local lessons upward
- Integrate company-wide efforts
- Modify the implementation themes
- Understand key obstacles to progress

CEO's End of Cycle Audit

- Study the results
- Evaluate and improve the planning process
- Identify issues for the next planning cycle
- Modify the planning process

smaller PDSA cycle for continuous improvement that takes place during the "Do" phase of the larger annual PDSA cycle of hoshin management. It provides feedback in a timely manner to ensure early rather than late corrective action. David Lord of Procter & Gamble explains:

> The monthly review is the self-diagnostic review. This review is conducted by the people who created the action plans and need to review progress with some frequency. While we recommend that these reviews occur monthly, ideally, it should be what is appropriate—daily, weekly, perhaps every two months if there are long lead times. Our request for monthly reviews is to encourage managers to get going and to check their progress on a regular basis. The self-diagnostic reviews do not require the boss to be present; the team does its own review. But the next level up from the team does need to make sure that the monthly reviews are getting done and whether subordinates are on schedule with their plan.

Many managers ask, "How should we structure the monthly review?" While there are a variety of formats, the reviews work best when they are brief and focused. The monthly review is not a time for posturing or parading. Rather, it is an opportunity to succinctly communicate actual progress against plan using facts and analysis.

Use a Standardized Format to Report Progress on a Monthly Basis

Some companies, such as Intel, encourage their employees to cover the agenda items shown in Figure 5.2. These guidelines are applicable at all levels of the hierarchy and for every level of abstraction.

Progress indicators report the current situation. A Gantt/milestone chart is typically used to show progress against schedule. Numerical indicators are displayed in a visual format to show progress against goals. Special attention is given to the numerical indicators to ensure that they (1) measure success appropriately, accurately, and consistently, (2) form a necessary and sufficient set to understand performance, (3) are cost effective, and (4) encourage behaviors that support overall performance.

Highlights include the key accomplishments and discoveries during the most recent period. Employees emphasize the quantitative impact of these results.

Figure 5.2. Use a system for documenting the reviews.

Progress Report

Plan Year: _____
Owner: _____
Revision Date: _____

Group strategic objective: 1.0 - Make our external upgrade PC boards first choice among IBM-compatible end users by achieving 95% VOC rating by Q1 (date).
Strategy: 1.1 - Deliver multimedia platforms to all customers in the available market; 80% of targetted design wins achieved by (date)

Highlights	Lowlights	Issues	Plans
• Voice product 25/33 platform development on schedule with beta-testing at five ISVs for second wave. • Data product 25/33 platform development released third product on schedule (Zeus-25x), producing five design wins in Q4 '93. • Field sales engineers (FSEs) have completed first of two technical training sessions for all geographies. • QA expenditures come in under target: $4.95.5k vs $528k.	• Video product 33/50 platforms slip projected at one quarter due to design bugs found in beta-testing. • Customer feedback process team slower than scheduled because documenting the AS-IS condition took longer than expected. • Factory yield is low on Zeus-25x output at 54%: incoming piece part problem a primary problem.	• Negotiation breakdown with three major customers (ABC, NBQ, XYZ) on establishing a uniform pricing policy. • Reorganization has created a need to fill five open requisitions during hiring freeze.	• Remove bugs in Video 33/50 platform and recover schedule. • Increase resource allocation of customer feedback process: define action plan in Q2. • Complete second technical training session for all FSEs in all geographies. • Resolve vendor problems dith defective piece parts. • Continue progress on Voice 25/33 platform and release second product (Adolby - 33XL).

Reprinted with permission of Intel Corporation. © Intel Corporation, 1995.

Lowlights describe the disappointments. Not all plans produce positive results. But information about failure is of equal importance to information about success. Lowlights are the less successful activities and results of the most recent period. Again, employees report the quantitative impact of these developments.

Issues refer to those obstacles that sometimes arise beyond the scope or control of the work team and influence the ability of the group to proceed. These barriers to progress (funding, time, personnel, etc.) can often by removed by senior management. Employees report any critical issues that are impeding progress.

Corrective action plans describe where the team intends to go from here. As events and obstacles develop, employees report their plans for corrective action, verify that all changes are aligned with other ongoing activities, and recommend issues to be considered in future rounds of planning.

A report on corrective action is a key differentiating characteristic of the hoshin review system. Specifically, this part of the review is designed to move the team from the "Study" phase of their micro PDSA cycle to the "Act" phase. In the context of hoshin management, teams do not merely monitor progress, they specify the mechanism to transfer their lessons into action.

Other companies, such as Hewlett-Packard, also use a standardized format to communicate progress. (See Figure 5.3.) In contrast, employees at Zytec use only three pieces of paper during the review. The cover sheet is the annual hoshin plan. The second sheet of paper is the implementation plan showing the objectives, goals, targets, indicators, and tools. The third sheet of paper is a visual display of the numerical indicators. John Rogers of Zytec observes:

> The second and third year, standardization was a big issue. We stayed away from the HP approach—nice forms and lots of detail. We probably suffered to some degree from that, but I would have had a difficult time forcing complex forms down people's throats. Instead, we basically have a single chart for each group that has their objective listed in a hoshin type matrix. . . . We added measurement techniques over on the right hand side. For each one of these charts, there are two other pages—one page is a chart or graph that tracks progress according to the measurements on the first page. This is presented during the hoshin review. The second page is a single-page action plan. The action plan is a communication tool for how the group is going to improve things.

Figure 5.3. The review summary sheet keeps the PDSA cycle rotating.

Legend   *
Trend   m: ▼▲ Change since last review
Concern   (c):   H High   M Moderate   L Low
Status   (s):   ○ On target ⊗ Behind plan ● Far below expectations ◑ Metrics or strategy change

Prepared by: J. Smith	Date:	Year:		Div:	Location: Quality Department
Objective/Strategy (P)	Actual Performance & Limits (D)	* S/C/T		Summary of Analysis of Deviations (C)	Implications for Future (A)

1. Customer Satisfaction
1.1 Timely resolution of customer issues
	Hot site response
	  Goal: < 22 days
	  Actual: 40 days
	  Limit: > 22 days
		◑		The measure has been based on time required for complete resolution. This depends too much on issue complexity	Measure time required to formulate a response plan for each hot site item. Set new goal

1.2 Timely, accurate, and appropriate answers to customer questions	Customer satisfaction index
	  Goal: 95%
	  Actual: 96%
	  Limit: 90%
		○
		▼
		H
				Index down slightly due to EDS turn around time (TAT). Impacted by multi-area "mega-job" from ICD	Monitor "mega-job" in future for TAT impact.

2. Commitment to our people
2.1 Insure a safe working environment by safety inspections
	# of unresolved safety issues without a plan.
	  Goal: 0
	  Actual: 2
	  Limit: 2
		⊗
		▼
		M
				Ownership of unresolved issues difficult to establish	Team of influencers formed to resolve issues. Team to also determine process for determining owner of future issues

	OSHA Case Rate
	  Goal: 0
	  Actual: 1 case
	  Limit: > 0
		●
		▼
		H
				Ergonomic injury due to heavy use of keyboards	Upgrade keyboards for heavy users
					Increase attention to job requirements versus individual abilities. Increase ergonomic safety training

PLAN	**DO**			**STUDY**	**ACT**

At Zytec, each manager presents his/her objectives to senior management on a monthly basis. A ten-minute time slot is allocated for each person. Most reviews can be easily accomplished within this time frame.

Use Facts and Analysis to Determine Corrective Actions

Whatever the specifics of the review meeting format, the key is to create a safe environment, one characterized by joint inquiry based

Review-Session Etiquette

- Manage by facts and analysis.
- Examine all deviations, positive and negative.
- Coach, don't police.
- Be an active listener. Ask clarifying questions. Try not to defend a position you have already taken.
- Accept confrontation without questioning the commitment of the confronting individual.
- Deliver unpleasant news in a non-threatening way.
- Emphasize inquiry over advocacy.
- Stay engaged in dialogue even when you do not get the answer you want.

on facts and analysis, not blame. Managers should act like coaches or facilitators, as opposed to dictators. An effective coach should:

- provide constructive feedback to maintain focus,
- remove barriers to progress,
- transfer knowledge and experience,
- provide resources, and
- recognize the team's contribution.

In a monthly review, results are the starting point. The emphasis is on the root cause analysis of deviations from plan in order to identify the necessary adjustments to the plan. (See Figure 5.4.) Even if the results are on plan, the team must verify that the results were achieved from the plan and not from some other phenomena. Observes John Rogers of Zytec:

> When we started MBP [management by planning], managers were concerned that the meetings would either become punitive ("Why didn't you achieve your objective this month?") or would become redundant, cursory, and a waste of time. None of these conditions happened. Zytec's CEO made it clear from the beginning that the purpose of the process is to disseminate successful ideas, tools, and techniques, and to provide a forum in which the manager can ask for help if help is needed to accomplish MBP objectives. Also, after three years of reporting, a natural rhythm developed. MBPs that are on track are dealt with quickly. Manag-

Figure 5.4. Employees use root cause analysis to determine corrective actions.

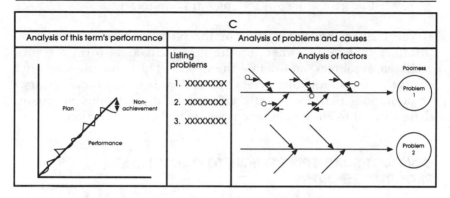

From *Hoshin Kanri: Policy Deployment for Successful TQM*, edited by Yoji Akao. English translation copyright © 1991 by Productivity Press, Inc., PO Box 13390, Portland,

ers who are orators by nature have become more succinct. Managers and (particularly) team members not accustomed to making presentations have developed more confidence with experience. All in all, the process has been a cultural benefit to the company by truly bringing our employees into the activities we use to effect change.

One last point: How can employees decide whether and in what way they should modify the plan? Three key questions include:

- Does this new opportunity support our current direction?
- What will we gain or lose by pursuing this opportunity?
- What we gain or lose by leaving our plans intact?

If you change the initial focus of the plan, then reevaluate your priorities. Assign an owner for the new focus area, form a team, reallocate resources, and define the details. Then communicate the change in direction so that others can modify their plans as necessary. Organizations that are directly affected by the revisions negotiate these changes to ensure alignment within and across functions.

CONDUCT QUARTERLY REVIEWS TO CONSOLIDATE PROGRESS REPORTS

The quarterly review is where the "hierarchy arrives" to see how the organization is performing. The quarterly review has four purposes:

- to study the effect of the action plan results on the strategy measures,
- to understand key obstacles and adjustments to the plan,
- to share learnings, and
- to seek help.

Quarterly reviews are not inspections. Rather they provide a vehicle for knowledge exchange. They channel local experiences and lessons upward in a consolidated and relevant format. David Lord explains:

Quarterly meetings are formal, even though we work hard to make them seem like work sessions. These sessions are where the hierarchy comes back in to see how everyone is doing on their important items. The hierarchy said earlier, "These are the important things to work on for me and the company; you need to help us put together the plans." So, now it is appropriate for the hierarchy to come back in and see how employees are doing. We look at results with a flag chart or a tree chart. And then we review any problems or adjustments to the plan that people had to make.

The quarterly review is not a "show and tell" experience. Instead, the emphasis is on understanding the capability of the system. Employees and their managers share problems, clarify messages, and explore gaps between desired outcomes and actual results. They use facts and analysis to reframe the "why" behind actions, not merely improve the "how."

Use a Flag System to Track Progress

Some tasks take longer that anticipated; other projects move more quickly. In hoshin management, both of these situations constitute a deviation from plan. Any significant deviation from plan needs to be identified and communicated up the hierarchy so that people can revise their assumptions and take corrective action.

There are several methods to track deviations from plan. Some companies (Milliken, for example) manage their planning system with minimal paper. The architecture of their total quality management system controls performance. Most other companies, however, use a visual tracking system, either on paper or by computer.

Hewlett-Packard uses a simple flag system to track performance throughout the year. (See Figure 5.5.) A flag signals the appropriate manager that something or someone needs attention. The appropriate parties can quickly focus on the problem and adjust activity to keep things on track. Meanwhile, the CEO and senior management team receive regular and frequent reports on progress. At any point in time, the CEO knows precisely what is working and how quickly the organization is making progress. Any deviation from plan that is critical at his level in the hierarchy receives focused attention.

Standardize the Quarterly Progress Report

While a quarterly review may sound simple to some people, for large corporations the choreography across levels, divisions, and geography can be quite intricate. Lois Gold of Hewlett-Packard describes that company's system:

On a quarterly basis, we have a formal roll up, right up to our executive committee. At each level, the manager reports on his or her whole plan. But you only go into detail on the exceptions. Each level of management is rolling up its piece of the plan, so the lower level stuff gets dropped off. By the time it gets to the president, he sees the stuff related to the three or four key strategies. It is very formal. There is a formal calendar

Figure 5.5. Hoshin/BFT review/response process flow.

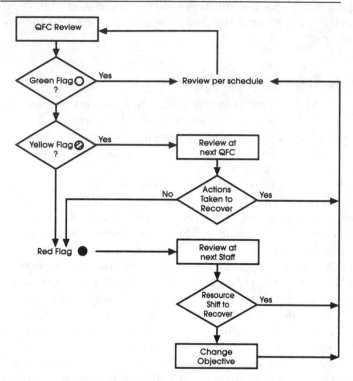

for it. In my organization, the review takes place over a six-week period. We start at the field level organization and roll it back up to my manager, so that he can do it for his review. In our case, it is geography that is the variable to get people together. We need 15 days to close our books so that everyone has the necessary data from all of the U.S., Latin America, and Canada, from district manager to regional manager to national sales manager, by segment to national manager to the geographic general manager. It is a four-week process from the time the books close. Our president gets his review of his hoshins in a rigorous way four times a year.

Hewlett-Packard documents and standardizes the feedback system using process maps and time lines. This increases the plan's reliability.

The HP quarterly reviews are a formal process. Starting at the lowest level of the organization, each manager reviews progress to date with direct reports. The focus is on deviations from plan. Cross-functional objectives are reviewed with peers. Each manager reviews his or her group results with the next higher level of management. This continues until results and unsolved issues are reviewed by top management.

CONDUCT AN ANNUAL AUDIT TO CONTINUALLY IMPROVE THE RELIABILITY OF THE PLANNING SYSTEM

The annual hoshin audit is more broad than the monthly and quarterly reviews. It goes beyond progress updates and corrective action to assess the performance of the entire planning system. Specifically, the chief executive officer conducts an end of cycle audit to:

- ensure that the strategic priorities were deployed and implemented in each department, and
- learn what is happening on the front line.

By evaluating the organization's strengths and weaknesses during each of the stages of the SA-PDSA cycle, the leadership creates an increasingly reliable strategic planning and implementation system.

Review Overall Progress at the End of the Cycle

In the annual review, the organization starts at the lowest level of the hierarchy that is affected by the hoshin plan. At that level, each manager reviews progress with his or her direct reports and peers. A consolidated report is shared with the next higher level of management. This continues until a final set of results and unresolved issues and opportunities is communicated to the top managers for their review. The emphasis during the annual review is not to boast, but to study those areas where deviations occurred.

Key elements of the annual review include:

- understanding the gap between expected results and actual progress to date,
- summarizing unresolved or emergent issues that may affect the next year's plan,

- documenting and standardizing what went *right* when expected results were achieved (in the form of flow charts, assumptions, protocols, practices, and procedures), and
- analyzing and finding the root cause of discrepancies.

The hoshin annual audit is used to shape the following year's plan. It helps the leadership understand the problems that members of the organization experienced when trying to implement the organization's policies. After all, there is little point in crafting new plans if the previous plans failed due to inadequate resources or an insincerity in planning.

Evaluate Skill at Using the Planning System

In addition to a progress review, hoshin companies conduct an annual self-assessment on their hoshin planning. Some companies, such as Intel, use the Malcolm Baldrige National Quality Award criteria to evaluate their organization. Other companies, such as SPA Resort Hawaiians, ask each department to use a numeric scale to rate itself on a variety of items: the alignment of department objectives with top management's hoshins, the deployment process, the gains achieved, and the like. In the deployment area, for example, a department would give itself 90 to 100 points if it has established a deployment system and has rotated through the PDSA cycles several times, 70 to 89 points if it has completed a PDSA cycle only once, 50 to 69 points if the department has specified methods for closing a gap, but not yet launched a full cycle, and so on.

Florida Power & Light also uses a disciplined review of its planning system to accelerate progress. Each year, deficiencies in the planning system are documented and addressed in the subsequent planning year. Figure 5.6 shows the evolution of this company's experience with implementation.

Zytec, too takes the time to isolate opportunities to improve their planning system. Observes John Rogers:

The first year, our challenge was to improve the quality of the employee suggestions. The second year, employees didn't chart particularly well or else they chose measurement objectives that didn't work too well. So, we chose to focus on that. The third year, we aimed to improve the process of creating a realistic action plan.

Figure 5.6. Document opportunities to improve the effectiveness of the strategy implementation system.

Policy Deployment Process Changes

Year	Changes	Remaining Problems
Prior to 1985	**MBO**	• MBO objectives were only cost-related but not met—rate case (1984)
1985	**EMBO pilot** • Department planning reviews • Departments established vision, fundamental objectives, and departmental objectives • Focus more than cost • Establish policy deployment committee (cost/budget)	• Only three departments involved • No corporate level reviews • No end-of-year review to check on how well process worked
1986	**EMBO-corporatewide** • Establish presidential reviews • Establish end-of-year policy deployment review • Sitcon 4/86 focused on policy deployment/87 plan (mid-term and long-term plan)	• Great number of projects not completed (51.7%)-time of review November 1986 (16.5%)-not until 1987 • Too many projects—each department required to have projects for each short-term plan • No focus on corporate issues • No executive-level coordination
1987	**Policy deployment-corporatewide** • Customers point of view • Business environment considered • Departments established targets and indicators for projects • Guidelines revised to reflect reduction in number of projects—policy deployment guidelines (6/86) • Policy deployment committee met to review all projects 8/86 for 1987 • End-of-year review became diagnosis • Assigned coordinating executive to each short-term plan • Required quality improvement story format (for 88 plan)	• Only 46% of policy deployment targets met • Departments not aligning their priorities to corporate objectives (to achieve customer satisfaction)
1988	• Implemented management reviews (levels I, II, III) • Aligned short-term plans to corporate indicators for quality elements (quality systems) • Defined role of short-term plan coordinating executives • Required master quality improvement story-format for control of short-term plan • Moved budget cycle to year end • Mini-sitcon coordinating executives now accountable to make targets • Formalized analysis from master quality improvement story reporting for each contribution	• 25% of targets not met • EFOR became unplanned for days off-line transmission forced outages • Nuclear energy equivalent availability • Short-term plan 2.1 - violations made overall, but Turkey Point failed • Alignment to quality elements off-cycle with table of tables update • Policy deployment actual versus target is too high
1989	• Formalized update procedure for table of tables to coincide with policy deployment calendar/policy deployment cycle • Established corporate format for "business plan" guidelines, standardized business plan process • Presidential review guidelines: -enhanced objectives to be more specific in the diagnosis of root cause (corporate level) -enhanced role of policy deployment committee to manage the action items from meetings -formalized action item process • Introduced quality/delivery and cost systems • Formalized cross-functional management	

Source: Bruce Sheridan. *Policy Deployment: the TQM Approach to Long-Range Planning.* Used by permission.

The annual review is the kickoff for the next round of planning. With "added intelligence," the leadership combines lessons from the prior year with potential issues for the next year to provide a sound strategy and implementation process. (Some companies invite outsiders or special counselors to participate in their annual reviews.) Reviewing provides a systematic way for individuals to examine their basic operating assumptions. What assumptions were made in good faith that later turned out to be inaccurate? What new assumptions will be pursued the next time around? Was the environment supportive of the learning process? The answers to these questions are essential to continuous improvement.

In summary, the hoshin audit system keeps activities aligned with the plan and the plan aligned with changes in the environment. A self-reinforcing and self-correcting planning system, hoshin management converts local lessons into new organizational maps. As objectives are achieved over time, new priorities are established based on the situation analysis. Such a rolling plan keeps the organization aligned with the evolving external and internal environment.

6

Create an Integrated Quality Management System

Today's organization is rapidly being transformed from a structure built out of jobs into a field of work needing to be done . . . people no longer take their cue form a job description or a supervisor's instructions. Signals come from the changing demands of the project. —William Bridges

Many people are thrilled when they see the power of hoshin planning. They see it as a management system to set priorities, allocate resources, and ensure faithful implementation.

But hoshin kanri is not for the fainthearted. Creating a hoshin management system is not so simple. It requires that managers and employees possess certain basic philosophies and capabilities. These include a focus on the long term, a market orientation, a participative management culture, process control, and a commitment to continuously improve all products and services.

These prerequisites fall within the general category of principles and practices described by the words "total quality management" (TQM), "total quality control" (TQC), or "continuous company-wide quality improvement" (CQI). The single most important aspect of this school of management is its emphasis on continuous quality improvement for customer delight.

Many people believe that the TQM system produces only *kaizen*, or incremental improvements in process performance. But this represents a fundamental misunderstanding of the word "continuous." Continuous improvement can and should be both incremental as well as breakthrough. Quality in daily work needs to generate continuous incremental improvement in processes fundamental to the existing business. Leaders also need to focus the organization on the vital few breakthrough requirements that will ensure a strategic position five to ten years down the road.

Companies vary in how they describe this larger TQM environment and the way in which hoshin management fits. Texas Instruments describes its comprehensive management model as having five interrelated components: customer first, teamwork, management by fact, excellence, and policy deployment (hoshin management). Hewlett-Packard describes its total quality system as including four cornerstones: customer focus, planning, process management, and an improvement cycle. Whatever the configuration, world class companies view the planning process as integral to their ability to achieve and maintain leadership status.

THE TQM MODEL FOR BUSINESS

In general, a total quality management environment is built around a specific set of principles, tools and techniques, and systems. TQM *principles* include such concepts as customer focus, employee empowerment, process control, continuous improvement, management by facts and analysis, and root cause problem solving.

These concepts form an integrated theory of management yet employees need practical tools to turn the theory into action. In a TQM environment, employees use special *techniques* to capture the voice of the customer, identify and eliminate the root cause of problems, and control unwanted process variation. These tools are applicable to problems arising in every function, not just manufacturing or engineering, and at every level of the hierarchy, shop floor to the executive suite. When these tools are viewed as a common language, members in one part of the organization can effectively communicate with others elsewhere in the company.

Philosophy and tools do not describe the extent of TQM. However, barriers in the form of company *systems* can deflect even the most skilled attempts to satisfy customer requirements. For this reason, certain business systems need to be created or modified to institutionalize TQM as a way of life. A TQM environment integrates among other things the customer information system, complaint handling system, suggestion system, employee performance appraisal system, quality assurance system, and objective setting system. These must be tailored to the organization's unique culture.

Hoshin planning is only one system among numerous planning systems that enable employees to act in the best interests of the organization. The financial planning system, the budgeting process, and the strategic planning process must be linked to create a seamless dynamic for continuous improvement.

Many managers insist that hoshin management is worth implementing, not simply because they get control of their strategic planning and implementation system, but also because it helps them drive the PDSA cycle and other tools for continuous improvement throughout their entire company. In the past, when employees complained that their managers did not use the TQM tools, senior managers often turned away. The leadership had no systematic way to force individuals to use the new tools. The hoshin management system forces managers to apply these tools on a regular basis, enabling them to develop their own capabilities as managers. It relies on all employees using tools like root cause analysis and process control to design and control their plans.

In summary, TQM is not something that you *do*; it's the way that you *manage*. Hoshin management is but one methodology to convert the theory to practice.

MANAGE THE BUSINESS FUNDAMENTALS IN ADDITION TO THE HOSHINS

"Well," you might be thinking, "hoshin management appears to provide a reliable system for achieving strategic breakthroughs. But what about the rest of the business? How do these two systems integrate?"

Hewlett-Packard calls these daily management issues *business fundamentals*. Procter & Gamble calls them *business essentials*. Whatever the vocabulary, most companies practicing hoshin management agree that the leadership must integrate the annual hoshin activities with quality in daily work. Observes Lois Gold of Hewlett-Packard:

> We were not successful with hoshin planning until we introduced the concept of daily management. People immediately saw the value of hoshin as a means to align the organization behind change and breakthrough, something they never had a mechanism for doing before. But others felt that it didn't address the many other things that they needed to pay attention to—in fact, a large part of their job. While we understood the concept of managing breakthrough objectives, we did not understand how significant business fundamentals or daily maintenance was to the whole system. In Japan, these efforts are really parallel processes: one deals with maintenance and monitoring the system, the other with breakthrough. They are both essential to understanding and managing the whole business. Today, the Hewlett-Packard manager's business plan includes the manager's annual hoshin plan as well as their business fundamentals. Together, these two plans provide a manager with all of the information he or she needs to run their business during that fiscal year.

Just because you select hoshins to mark key areas for concentrated effort, this doesn't mean that you can ignore the activities related to maintaining your current system. Hoshin management ensures that you will be in business tomorrow. Business fundamentals are critical to the health of the business today. Continuous improvement has both an incremental component and a breakthrough component.

Use a Business Fundamentals Table to Document Commitments to Process Improvement

Hewlett-Packard plans separately for these two types of activity by using two different planning tables. The company uses a hoshin deployment matrix (described in Chapter 3) to document the manager's commitment to support the breakthrough objectives. A separate document records the daily management priorities for key business processes. (See Figure 6.1 for an example of a business fundamentals planning table.) The strategic breakthrough objectives and business fundamentals are reviewed on a regular basis.

Apart from the hoshin plan, the manager is responsible for each key business process, ensuring that:

Figure 6.1. Use a planning table to manage business fundamentals.

Prepared by: J. Smith		Date:	Fiscal year:	Division:	Location/Department: Quality	
Strategy		Target/Goal & Limits		Review period	Date source (Reporter)	Owner

1. Customer satisfaction
  1.1 Timely resolution of
     customer issues
		Hot Site Response
		  Goal: ≤ 22 days
		  Limit: > 22 days
				Monthly	Q&R Report	R. Jones

1.2 Timely, accurate and
     appropriate answers
     to customer questions
		Customer Satisfaction Index
		  Goal: 95%
		  Limit: < 90%
				Monthly	Customer Satisfaction Report	F. Hall

2. Commitment To Our People
  2.1 Insure safe working
     environment by safety
     inspections
		Number of unresovled safety
		issues without a plan
		  Goal: 0
		  Limit: > 2
				Monthly	Safety Inspection Report	J. Smith

		OSHA Case Rate
		  Goal: 0
		  Limit: > 0
				Monthly	Safety Report	J. Smith

- It is understood.
- It is documented.
- It is standardized throughout the organization.

Daily management tables typically include certain pieces of critical information. This information aims to:

- Identify metrics for customer satisfaction
- Identify the key business processes that deliver customer requirements
- Establish process targets and/or control values
- Develop employees to improve and control these processes
- Study results and standardize
- Document financial performance

The daily management tables are applicable to every function within the company. Progress is reviewed on a weekly, monthly, and quarterly basis. (See Figure 6.2 for a business fundamentals review table.)

USE HOSHIN MANAGEMENT TO DRIVE REENGINEERING

Quality in daily work is not the only set of employee activities that needs to be integrated with the hoshin planning system. Another set of activities is cross-functional in nature. These activities generally center on cross-functional processes that relate to quality, cost, delivery, safety, morale, and new product development. This is the horizontal component of management alluded to in the ship analogy at the beginning of this book.

While some horizontal business processes may already satisfy customers and employees, others can benefit from a complete rethinking. In their best selling book, *Reengineering the Corporation*, Michael Hammer and James Champy stress that many companies need to redesign their business systems based on changing customer requirements and advances in technology. The trick is to figure out

Figure 6.2. Use a standard format for reviewing business fundamentals.

* Legend	Status (S):	O Meets Goal	Concern (C):	H High (explain)	Trend (T):	↑ Right Direction
		◐ Meets Limit		M Moderate (explain)		
		● Worse than Limit		L Low (good job!)		↓ Wrong Direction
		⊙ Metrics/Goal Change				

Prepared by:		Review Date:		Year:	Location:
Item/ Performance Measure	Goal - Limit - Actual	*S/C/T	Summary of Results or Deviations	Implications for the Future	

which are those critical processes and how to manage the redesign activity and still keep the business running.

Reengineering does not eliminate the need for hoshin management. Choosing to reengineer a particular business process may emerge as a breakthrough strategy using the hoshin priority setting process. Lord of Procter & Gamble goes on to observe:

> I put reengineering under the umbrella of TQM. Typically, reengineering is done on horizontal systems. But the Japanese say, before you get into cross-functional management you better be pretty good at daily management and vertical management. And vertical management is hoshin management.

Reengineering typically focuses on the horizontal business systems within the organization. The decision to reengineer a process still needs to be driven from a thorough analysis of the external environment, e.g., the first phase of the hoshin planning process. Hoshin management specifies where the breakthrough gaps are. Reengineering is one possible means to close the gap.

Hoshin management is a mechanism to orchestrate organizational changes. It has a built-in flexibility that rallies the troops to accomplish what needs to be done, not necessarily what is easy to do. When the leadership goes to deploy a vital breakthrough objective, it may discover that the current organization structure does not provide the means. This is not a problem for the hoshin management system. Using the deployment process, specifying the means, measures and owners, the company can redesign itself. Observes Warren Evans of Intel,

> We decided to be driven by the situation analysis of the hoshin planning process rather than the existing organizational structure. The situation analysis of the hoshin planning system shapes the target. Then we look to see if we have the means to deploy the target. If we don't have the means, then we reorganize to achieve the target. In this way, the situation analysis of the hoshin system drives our organizational structure. Employees can see the logic of the direction of the business and whether or not they or their activities fit in.

Intel uses the situation analysis and the rigor of the hoshin planning process to direct organizational redesign.

In short, hoshin management *is* change management. It is a

system to focus the organization on a few customer-centered priorities critical to establishing a strategic position three to five years down the road. It is a system to steer members of the organization in a direction different from where they are headed today.

INTEGRATE HOSHIN PLANNING WITH THE INDIVIDUAL PERFORMANCE REVIEW

So how does the individual get evaluated in a hoshin environment, especially when the hoshin deployment process depends on teamwork? The hoshin audit described in Chapter 5 focuses on the capability of the planning and implementation system. Yet, many companies still feel the need to evaluate individual performance.

This is not a trivial problem. Today, many organizations are struggling with the traditional concept of "the job." While the job, as we know it, is a familiar and secure concept, more and more organizations are finding that it simply no longer fits the reality of their business environment. (For an insightful discussion of this change, see William Bridges' article, "The End of the Job," *Fortune*, September 19, 1994, pp. 62–74.)

Rather, projects and teamwork are the name of the game. In a rapidly changing environment, responsibilities change quickly. An employee is often assigned to a new task well before a prior project is finished. On an on-going basis, an employee is expected to support different team leaders, keep different schedules, manage relationships in different locations, and perform different tasks.

Hoshin management helps in this environment. In companies that practice hoshin management, people no longer take direction from a job description or their functional boss. Rather, they respond to changes in the environment. Employees focus their unique energies and collective resources on the vital few strategic gaps that must be closed. As the challenges change, so do their objectives, strategies, measures, and goals.

Many companies use their employee performance appraisal system to support the hoshin management process. At Hewlett-Packard, each person has a position plan with standards or targets. Some of these targets are related to a set of business fundamentals that a particular person owns, others relate to their annual hoshin commitments.

The Semiconductor Group at Texas Instruments also links its hoshin management system to the appraisal system. Observes Ron McCormick,

> We used policy deployment for several years before we tied everybody's performance reviews to the policy deployment process. We changed the entire performance appraisal process. We used to have a check list covering such things as attendance, quality, teamwork, etc. Now, we have a process that asks: What are your committed projects in support of the policy deployment priorities? That is the key part of the performance appraisal process. We probably took too long to make these changes. If the policy deployment process identifies the most important priorities for the company, and you deploy these to the organization, and people develop the tactics to make them happen, then the appraisal process shouldn't be focused on some different set of things.

Hoshin management needs the support of the human resources function. In the early stages of hoshin management, human resource personnel may believe that their existing evaluation process is supportive of the hoshin process. But, internal customer satisfaction surveys eventually lead the human resource managers to conclude that the traditional performance appraisal is poorly linked with the key business priorities of the organization. Rather, it often has its own agenda.

Many companies link their employee appraisal system with the hoshin deployment system. Yet this does not mean that employees are penalized for missed targets. What is most important to evaluate is whether employees are *participating* in the planning process, improving their skills as team players, working to improve their skills in communication, planning, and problem solving—all the *behaviors* by which the organization hopes to achieve its desired results. Again, the emphasis is on the process, not just the results.

WORK TOWARD HOSHIN MANAGEMENT

Some companies are well on their way to creating an organization focused on continuous improvement. Others are just beginning the journey.

There are three phases of moving towards a TQM practice. These are:

Belief. Early in the transition phase, members of the organization learn about, adopt, and internalize the basic principles of TQM as the core of their management philosophy.

Capability. To turn the theory into action, employees must acquire, apply, and build capability around the skills, tools, and techniques needed in this new environment. These include the PDSA cycle for continuous improvement, root cause analysis, and process control.

Alignment. Finally, the leadership must link jobs and tasks to the overall goals and objectives of the organization so that work proceeds in a coordinated fashion—People, processes, and business systems must integrate in a seamless dynamic.

Some leaders may be disappointed with hoshin management if they fail to first orient and train their employees in these tools and techniques. For them, hoshin management will not produce the dramatic results that they expected. This is because they attempt to implement hoshin management (an alignment tool) before employees are committed during the orientation phase and are given the skills and capabilities to take action. To succeed at hoshin management, the leadership must build the basic capabilities associated with total quality management.

Does this mean that an organization can not introduce hoshin management until employees are oriented and have acquired the necessary skills? The answer is no! The leadership can begin to introduce certain aspects of the hoshin management system. But full implementation and skill with this planning tool generally comes after several iterations of the planning cycle.

Start by Mapping Your Own Planning System

As with all good process management, process redesign begins with getting a grip on your existing processes and protocol. The same is true for strategic planning and implementation system.

Before you modify your existing planning system, draw a map of it. Take the time to identify defects. Map the various pieces, inputs, and calendar aspects of your current process to figure out where to start. Some companies attempt to skip this step. They say that they have no strategic planning process. In most cases, some kind of process exists, however informal it might be.

So, take the time to study the situation. Create an open and safe setting to review the planning process. If senior managers fear recrimination, they may be reluctant to candidly report the extent to which they currently manage their plans. Emphasize the need to identify opportunities for improvement.

Practice Makes Perfect

Many people ask, how long does hoshin planning take? How much time does it consume? The answer is that it is different for every organization. A small organization in crisis may call all relevant parties together and hammer out plans over a period of several weeks. Another organization may require a planning process that extends over a period of several months. Regardless of the circumstances, you can never achieve breakthroughs quickly or lazily.

The very fact that there is no single "This is how to do it, so now go do it" aspect of hoshin management is disconcerting to many managers. Many people believe, "If it isn't something that I can figure out in one day or delegate in a three-hour meeting, then it is a waste of my time." But think about this for a minute. What if you can't change the systems and behaviors of your organization in an instant? What if the intrinsic nature of strategic breakthrough is that you've got to devote a lot of time inquiring, studying, analyzing, and coordinating with others? Is it worth giving up on the management system just because you would rather take a shortcut? Observes Warren Evans of Intel,

> I initially went out and did my research. I collected examples from a variety of U.S. and Japanese companies that were using this system. Then I backward engineered the material to distill the information to a set of basic principles. Then I built it back up again based on the Intel culture, using the language of Intel, not that of the sample companies. Today, our process is continually evolving.

Quite simply, the length of time that it takes to specify and validate detailed action plans is why most organizations fail to make strategic breakthroughs at all. Chuckles Evans,

> Three years ago, we considered our hoshin management system proprietary. But then we discovered that most people [in other organizations] can't do it anyway. They do not take the time to figure out the basic principles of this system and then adapt it to their unique culture.

In other words, being aware of this system is not a competitive advantage. *Adapting, implementing, and improving the system is.* Coordination and alignment are hard work. Whereas organizational charts are relatively easy to change, aligning people, activities, resources, and performance metrics is a different matter.

Learning how to implement policy deployment is like learning to ride a bike. At first it can be awkward. You spend a lot of time concentrating on keeping your balance. When you finally acquire the skill, you no longer think about it. Instead, you concentrate on your destination and observe the milestones along the way.

The same is true for hoshin planning. The first year is apt to feel awkward, and at times, frustrating. However, as managers and subordinates learn what to expect and how to work together, the planning process becomes more comfortable, the cycle time shortens, and reliability improves. In the end, strategy implementation is a process, and just like any other process, it can be systematically improved. Ron McCormick advises:

> You can't study this thing forever and get it right the first time. The whole idea of determining what's important, deploying it, and involving the people is an evolutionary process that has to fit the culture of the company. So, get some training—don't do the obvious things wrong. Then just get started and say "we are going to do this a couple of years and figure out how it works." Then take some surveys of the people who have used the process, including the staff and support organizations. See how it's working, and make improvements based on their suggestions.

As you reduce the planning cycle time, the organization becomes more adept and accurate in its outcomes. It can respond more quickly to changes in the environment. And increased responsiveness yields a competitive edge. But reduced cycle time requires that you get better at communicating, setting realistic targets, selecting appropriate indicators, and monitoring and correcting deviations from plan.

In the end, hoshin management is a system for time management. It brings discipline to the overall management of the company. It gives the leadership specific tools and methodologies to reliably communicate and execute a change in direction. A disciplined system for activity and control, it focuses collective energy on those things that matter most to the organization.

Appendix A

Statistical Tools

Figure A.1. Analytic tools organize and display numeric data.

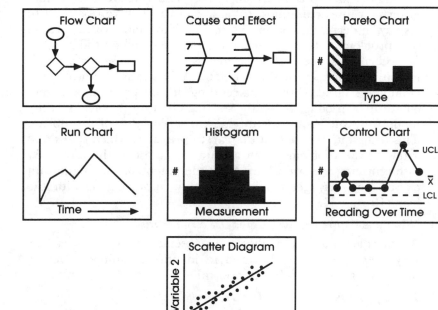

1. **Where are the data?** *Use a checksheet.*

   A checksheet is a form that facilitates the collection of data to clarify the nature of a problem being solved. It can be used quickly and easily to compile data in a format that can be used later for quantitative analysis. Data are collected using ticks, check marks, or numbers to measure things or to record how often something happens in a given time period. A checksheet is frequently used to gather data on defective items, defect locations, and defect causes.

2. **With what frequency are problems occurring?** *Use a histogram.*

   A histogram is a bar graph showing the frequency of occurrence of a measured characteristic. The variation of observations is called the distribution of variable data. A histogram is used to make decisions about where to focus initial improvement efforts. It is useful for visually communicating information about a process and helping to make decisions about where to focus improvement efforts.

3. **Which problems are most prevalent?** *Use a Pareto chart.*

   A Pareto chart sorts raw data into several categories and rank ordering causes from most to least significant. It can be used to display, in decreasing order, the relative importance of each cause of a problem. Relative contribution may be based on the number of occurrences, the cost associated with each cause, or another measure of impact on the problem. A line graph indicates the cumulative value of the data, ending at 100 percent. A Pareto chart can be used to choose the starting point for problem solving, monitoring success, or identifying the basic cause of a problem. This technique is based on the Pareto principle, which states that a few of the problems often account for most of the effect. By distinguishing the critical few from the potentially less significant causes, you may get maximum quality improvement with the least effort.

4. **What has happened over time?** *Use a run chart.*

   A run chart is a graphic display of observed data points as they vary over time. It can be used to identify meaningful trends, patterns, or shifts in behavior over time.

5. **Is the process in control?** *Use a control chart.*

   A control chart is a run chart that has control limit lines at the top, bottom, and middle of the display. It is used to detect whether variation in data is due to the inevitable variations that occur under normal conditions or to a specific cause or abnormal condition.

6. **What are the contributing factors?** *Use a fishbone diagram.*

A fishbone diagram is a visual representation of the relationships between a given effect and its potential causes. It can be used to identify, explore, and display the possible causes of a specific problem or condition (effect). A well-detailed cause and effect diagram will take the shape of a fishbone, hence its name. The problem or effect to be analyzed is written at the right, where the fish's head would be. The factors that contribute to the effect are written as branches directly attached to the main trunk. Smaller branches fanning out from them represent specific influences within each major cause.

7. **Is there a correlation?** *Use a scatter diagram.*

A scatter diagram is used to display what happens to one variable when another variable changes. It can be used to test a theory that the two variables are related. Scatter diagrams cannot be used to prove that changes in one variable cause changes in another variable, but they can identify whether a relationship exists and the strength of that relationship.

8. **What does the process look like?** *Use a process flow diagram.*

A process flow diagram is a pictorial representation of the steps in any work process. It is used to investigate opportunities for improvement in any process, including production processes, administrative processes, or the flow of information or services. By examining how various steps in a process relate to each other, you can uncover potential sources of trouble. A process flow diagram is used to identify actual and ideal paths that any product or service follows, allowing deviations to be highlighted. It can be applied to any segment of a process to serve as the basis of process documentation.

Appendix B

Management and Planning Tools

Figure B.1. Seven management and planning tools help to organize language data.

General Planning	Intermediate Planning	Detailed Planning

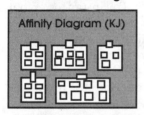

Affinity Diagram (KJ)

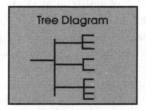

Tree Diagram

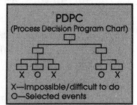

PDPC
(Process Decision Program Chart)

X—Impossible/difficult to do
O—Selected events

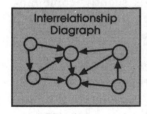

Interrelationship Diagraph

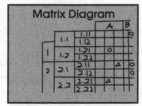

Matrix Diagram

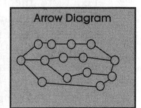

Arrow Diagram

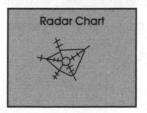

Radar Chart

1. What are the major concerns or issues? *Use an Affinity Chart.*

When we first begin to plan, there are many ideas and levels of aggregation. Among the various thoughts, opinions, and concerns, there are potentially hidden and insightful relationships. Unfortunately, we are often trapped in our past logic. We become blind to evolving structures as our environment changes. The affinity chart helps us to organize issues and concerns in a creative way. By grouping similar elements, we can identify natural and often new relationships among issues.

When to use it:

To organize customer or employee concerns.
To simplify the issues.
To create a fresh approach to describe a set of concerns.
To achieve consensus on the issues.
To identify patterns among seemingly unrelated factors.

How to use it:

1. Articulate a single question and place it before the group. Keep the question as non-prejudicial as possible. For instance: "What are the customer concerns?"
2. Brainstorm ideas. Do not criticize or edit the contributions at this stage. Record ideas exactly as they are communicated.
3. Put all bits of information on 3 × 5 cards or 3M Post-It notes.
4. Group similar ideas or pieces of information by physically moving the cards. In many cases, this step is done silently, i.e., team members rearrange the cards silently, combining thoughts with an affinity for one another, until everyone feels comfortable with the grouping. Eliminate any redundant cards.
5. Establish "header," or title cards for each group of common ideas. Write each title as a short "noun-verb" phrase.
6. If there are more than ten different cards in a grouping, create another level of aggregation. In other words, look for a finer distinction. Set aside "loner cards" and give them their own heading.

Outcome: A set of relationships grouped by common theme.

2. **Which factor causes or influences another one?** *Use an Interrelationship Diagraph.*

Many problems emerge from an interacting system of complex variables. To begin to solve the "mess," we must try to identify those factors that are the root cause, or drivers, of the dynamic situation. The interrelationship diagram, sometimes called the relations diagram, can be used to identify the critical factors, drivers, or root cause(s) of a systemic problem. Using the same bits of information in the affinity chart, the interrelationship diagram can help us to identify, analyze, and classify the cause and effect relationships among a complex set of issues.

When to use it:

To display the cause and effect relationships when the system is too complex for a fishbone diagram.

To separate symptoms from root causes.

To sequence management issues.

To identify bottleneck factors in the environment.

To identify the most serious problem areas.

How to use it:

1. Phrase a single question and place it before the team, e.g., "What are the driving elements in this situation?"
2. Place groupings from the affinity chart, the "header cards," in a circle or network.
3. Pick one element. Look for a possible relationship between this item and every other item. Draw a one-way arrow to indicate whether this item influences, or is influenced by, each of the other items. If there is a two-way relationship, record only the stronger of the two.
4. Repeat Step 3 for each of the other elements.
5. For each element, count the number of arrows going in (I). Then count the number of arrows going out (O).
6. Look for patterns of arrows to identify key causes or factors. Items with a significantly larger number of O's than I's indicate that this factor is a driver. Draw a line around these factors. Any items with a large number of incoming arrows are also worthy of further attention.

Outcome: A map of the cause and effect relationships, including the key drivers or the outcomes of an effective solution.

3. What is our relative progress in key categories of performance?
Use a Radar Chart.

When we set priorities, it is sometimes useful to know where we stand in relation to our ideal state. It can be advantageous to focus our efforts where there are large gaps in performance. The radar chart is a single graphic that displays the size of the gaps between the current level of performance and the ideal state in a variety of performance gaps.

When to use it:

To map the relative performance progress against every and all elements of a vision.
To display strengths and weaknesses.
To compare current reality with the ideal state.
To display important categories of performance.

How to use it:

1. Begin with key themes. These may be the "header" cards from the affinity chart.
2. Place the cards in a circle on a large surface.
3. Emanating from the center of the cards, draw a line to each card. The results will be a picture that looks like spokes on a wheel.
4. View each spoke as a ruler to measure progress.
5. Create a scale on each spoke from "0" at the center to "100" at the tip of the spoke. The value "100" represents the achievement of the element or goal represented by that spoke.
6. Reach consensus on the relative progress towards each element. In other words, answer the question: "Where are we today along the spectrum of fully realizing our desired state for this element?"
7. Mark each spoke accordingly. Numerical accuracy is less important than directionality.
8. Connect the dots, i.e., the status points, to create a radar-like pattern.
9. Analyze the set of gaps to further inform your selection of one element upon which to focus.

Outcome: A map of the relative gaps between current performance and the ideal state for key vision elements.

4. What needs to be addressed to achieve this goal? *Use a Tree Diagram.*

The tree diagram translates a single goal or purpose into increasingly detailed actions. The tree diagram is similar to the fishbone diagram and visually resembles it.

When to use it:

To determine the root cause(s).
To sequence a set of tasks.
To move from the big picture to the details.
To identify gaps in logic.
To examine the logical link among tasks.
To understand what needs to be accomplished.
To translate general needs into operational requirements.
To explore all possible means to address key problem areas.
To deploy broad objectives into specific activities.

How to use it:

1. Begin with one simple statement to describe the issues, concerns, problem, or goal.
2. Brainstorm all possible tasks, methods, or causes that answer the question, "To achieve x, what must occur or exist?" Some of these ideas can be taken from the affinity chart.
3. Record the answers on 3×5 cards.
4. Place the overall goal or purpose on the left.
5. Ask the question, "What task do we need to complete to achieve this goal or purpose?" Write all answers in a short "noun-verb" phrase. Sort and select answers from the remaining cards and place them to the right of the central issue.
6. Repeat step 5 for each task placed next to the central issue. If none of the cards answer the question, create a new card, or cards, and continue. Repeat the process until all the cards are placed on the tree diagram, and all tasks are specified to the appropriate level of detail.
7. Double-check the logic of the tree diagram by starting at the right with the most basic task, asking the question, "If we do these things, will we accomplish the next task/goal?"
8. Review with others to identify inconsistencies or omissions.

Outcome: A map of the full range of tasks or paths needed to accomplish a primary goal and related sub-goals.

5. Which things and people do we need to implement this plan? *Use a Matrix Diagram.*

The matrix diagram visually displays the relationships between two sets tasks, functions, or characteristics. When one series of characteristics is arranged in a horizontal row, and another series of characteristics are placed in a vertical column, visual symbols at the intersections will indicate the strength of the relationship.

When to use it:

To compare two or more sets of items and identify their relationships.

To compare potential action plans with criteria.

To compare all possible means with broad target areas.

To match departments/functions with objectives and means to choose the best options.

To match possible actions with key objectives to choose the best options.

To compare alternative courses of action.

How to use it:

1. Generate two or more sets of items that will be compared in the matrix. (These may emerge from the last row of a tree diagram.)
2. Label each axis.
3. Place one set of items on one axis of the matrix. The other set goes on the remaining axis. In other words, list each set of items in their appropriate row or column.
4. Draw lines to form boxes at the intersection of each paired set of items.
5. For each pair of items, select a symbol to describe the nature of the relationship. If there is no relationship, leave the cell blank.
   Responsibility (Direct responsibility, Indirect responsibility, Consensus)
   Importance (Most critical, More critical, Critical)
   Progress (In process, Scheduled, Evaluation possible)
6. Record the legend for the symbol system that is selected.
7. Analyze the completed chart to identify patterns and omissions.

Outcome: A map of the strength of the relationships between two or more sets of information.

6. How can we plan the introduction of a new initiative? *Use a PDPC.*

PDPC is a contingency planning tool. The PDPC, or Process Decision Program Chart, helps you to plan something you are doing for the first time. It helps you to pre-think what might go wrong, and identify appropriate countermeasures.

When to use it:

When the goal, problem or process is an unfamiliar one.
To identify errors or gaps in a plan prior to its implementation.
To prevent errors.

How to use it:

1. Start with a purpose. In the case of a tree diagram, take the most important initial branch of the tree diagram (i.e., start with an item to the immediate right of the ultimate goal). Ask the questions, "What could go wrong at this step?" or "What other path could this step take?"
2. List the answers, e.g., "Problems," by branching off the original path of the tree diagram. Insert the possible problems into the tree diagram sequence. If the answers are prepared on cards, they can be moved easily.
3. For each answer, ask, "What could we do to prevent this from happening?" List possible counteractions and countermeasures. Enclose these countermeasures in "clouds."
4. Continue with this process until this original branch of the tree diagram is exhausted.
5. Repeat these steps with the next most important branch.
6. Continue until all original branches of the tree diagram are exhausted.
7. Assemble the detailed branches into a final PDPC diagram.
8. Review with appropriate parties.
9. Identify those countermeasures that have already been implemented or solved. For each remaining counteraction, note its "doability" or when it will be implemented. Focus on those that have not been addressed.

Outcome: A contingency plan for a new initiative.

7. **How can we manage simultaneous requirements?** *Use an Activity Network Diagram/Arrow Diagram.*

To map simultaneous activities, we can use an arrow diagram—a simple tool which visually maps a recurring process. This tool is closely related to CPM (Critical Path Method) and PERT (Program Evaluation and Review Technique) diagrams.

When to use it:

To schedule and control parallel tasks in an effective manner.
When subtasks, their sequencing, and duration are well known.
When the process has a well documented history such as in new product development, construction projects, and marketing.
To map a complex system.
To reveal the most critical paths for a plan to meet its deadline.

How to use it:

1. List all necessary tasks to complete the project. Write these tasks on the upper half of a 3 × 5 card. Draw a line across the middle of the card.
2. Shuffle the cards and spread out in a random order on a large table.
3. Look for sequencing relationships among the cards. Place cards in order to reflect these relationships. Pay attention to parallel tasks or series of tasks. Number the tasks.
4. Flag the beginning and end of each parallel path with nodes. Nodes are symbols that mark the beginning and ending points of an extended task or event. Number the nodes and place arrows between tasks within a path as well as arrows to connect paths to one another.
7. Study and record the number of hours, days, weeks, months, etc. for each task. Record the time on the bottom half of the card.
8. Calculate the earliest and latest start time for each node. The earliest node time is when the job can be started; the latest node time is when the job must be completed. Calculate the longest cumulative path to identify the total project completion time.

Outcome: A map of the most efficient path and realistic schedule of tasks to complete a project.

About the Author

Michele L. Bechtell is president of PIXIS Inc., a Cambridge-based management consulting and training firm dedicated to curriculum development for organizational change and strategy deployment. Previously, Ms. Bechtell served as a senior management consultant for Athur D. Little, Inc., an international management and technology consulting firm, and the Forum Corporation, a human resource management training company. Her first book, *Untangling Organizational Gridlock: Strategies for Building a Customer Focus* (1993) was co-published by AMACOM Books and ASQC Quality Press.

OTHER AMA MANAGEMENT BRIEFINGS OF INTEREST

Blueprints for Service Quality: The Federal Express Approach, SECOND EDITION

Detailed, how-to information on personnel practices and quality measurement systems at Federal Express. Recently updated. Stock #02356XSPR, $11.25 AMA Members/$12.50.

Quality Alone Is Not Enough

Puts quality improvement programs into perspective and provides tools for measuring quality, linking time and quality, and achieving the shortest path to quality. Stock #02349XSPR, $11.65 AMA Members/$12.95.

Blueprints for Continuous Improvement: Lessons from the Baldrige Winners

Examines the strategies, tools, and techniques used by companies that have won the Baldrige Quality Award in recent years. Stock #02352XSPR, $11.25 AMA Members/$12.50.

The New Teamwork: Developing and Using Cross-Function Teams

Organizations need teamwork within departments as well as between departments. This briefing explains why a broader kind of teamwork is necessary and presents "tools" for building a "team-based" organization. Stock #02353XSPR, $11.25 AMA Members/$12.50.

Complete the **ORDER FORM** on the following page. For faster service, **CALL** or **FAX** your order.

PERIODICALS ORDER FORM

(Discounts for bulk orders of five or more copies).

Please send me the following:

☐ ____ copies of **The Management Compass: Steering the Corporation Using Hoshin Planning,** Stock #2358XSPR, $17.95 AMA Members/$19.95.

☐ ____ copies of **Blueprints for Service Quality: The Federal Express Approach, SECOND EDITION,** Stock #02356XSPR, $11.25 AMA Members/$12.50.

☐ ____ copies of **Quality Alone Is Not Enough,** Stock #02349XSPR, $11.65 AMA Members/$12.95.

☐ ____ copies of **Blueprints for Continuous Improvement: Lessons from the Baldrige Winners,** Stock #02352XSPR, $11.25 AMA Members/$12.50.

☐ ____ copies of **The New Teamwork: Developing and Using Cross-Function Teams,** Stock #02353XSPR, $11.25 AMA Members/$12.50.

Name: _____

Title: _____

Organization: _____

Street Address: _____

City, State, Zip: _____

Phone: (   ) _____

Signature: _____

Please add appropriate sales tax and include $3.75 for shipping and handling.

☐ Payment enclosed.   ☐ Bill me.

AMA'S NO-RISK GUARANTEE: If for any reason you are not satisfied, we will credit the purchase price toward another product or refund your money. No hassles. No loopholes. Just excellent service. That is what AMA is all about!

AMA Publication Services
P.O. Box 319
Saranac Lake, NY 12983